"I have long considered Dr. Mat ⟨...⟩ passionate, genuine, and contagious evangelists. In his new book, *Mobilize to Evangelize*, he gives pastors, staff, and churches an incredible tool to help them assess their present state of evangelism and develop a more robust theology and philosophy of evangelism. More importantly, as you read and consider this tool, you will certainly grow in your burden and passion for the equipping of the saints for the work of the ministry in the discipline of evangelism."

—*Tommy Kiker, Associate Professor of Pastoral Theology, Southwestern Baptist Theological Seminary*

"A pastor has many duties and, if he is to be effective, he must know what God's Word says about his assignment. Of all the responsibilities assigned to a pastor, perhaps none is more important than setting the tone for evangelistic effectiveness. If the pastor is evangelistic, the people will be evangelistic. If the pastor has a heart for the lost, his heart will eventually become the heart of the congregation. Thus, the pastor sets the temperature for evangelism in the local church. He is more than a thermometer; he is a thermostat.

"In *Mobilize to Evangelize*, my friend Dr. Matt Queen gives practical and resourceful ways for pastors to increase the evangelistic thermostat in their churches and stay hot on the trail for lost souls. Every pastor needs this book in his library. Your congregation will thank you for it."

—*Daniel Dickard, pastor, Friendly Avenue Baptist Church, Greensboro, North Carolina*

"*Mobilize to Evangelize* is an excellent resource for church leaders and congregations to assess evangelistic effectiveness. Accurate assessment is needed in order to formulate and implement an achievable strategy. All who desire to passionately proclaim the Gospel and see people follow Jesus as His disciples will do well to consider this challenging work."

—*Seth Polk, lead pastor, Cross Lanes Baptist Church, Cross Lanes, West Virginia*

"Pastor, *Mobilize to Evangelize* will guide you and your leadership team to implement a strong and biblically based evangelism program in your church. In this book, Matt Queen provides a fantastic assessment tool to find the current evangelistic temperature of your congregation and encourage you with the next steps to launch a powerful outreach strategy. This book is the launching point to set your people on mission to reach the lost in your community!"

—*Anthony Svajda, senior pastor, Harvey Baptist Church, Stephenville, Texas*

"Evangelism is one of those great disciplines about which everyone talks, but sadly, very few actually do. When I ask believing leaders why they don't actively evangelize, most of them have the want-to, they just don't know practical ways to get started. Nevertheless, this incredible book by Dr. Matt Queen is a helpful tool to get the church back to working as witnesses for Christ. Matt is the real deal when it comes to setting an example for us all in sharing our faith. He says it, does it, and lives it. May the Lord use him and this book to teach us all how to *mobilize to evangelize* for the glory of God!"

—*Shane Pruitt, director of evangelism, Southern Baptists of Texas Convention*

"After using Dr. Queen's *Everyday Evangelism* for years, I am thrilled to see him release *Mobilize to Evangelize*. More than a plea to share the Gospel, this is a workbook for pastors who want to assess current church evangelism culture and develop a functional plan for recovery and health. Pastor, you will finish this book with a strategy that fits your church!"

—*Shawn Nichols, pastor, Wilmont Place Baptist Church, Oklahoma City, Oklahoma*

"*Mobilize to Evangelize* provides pastors pointed means to assess their current evangelistic challenges and proven direction to move them forward to effective evangelism. Every pastor and staff member should study this work carefully and use it to move forward into the local community with the Gospel."

—*David Mills, senior pastor, Beech Haven Baptist Church, Athens, Georgia*

"Evangelism is one of the most important tasks of the local church, yet many churches are struggling to reach their communities for Christ. *Mobilize to Evangelize* addresses this issue head-on by giving a practical tool that not only assesses your church's philosophy and practice of evangelism, but also guides your church through the process of correcting any evangelistic deficiencies and strengthening any evangelistic efficiencies. Matt Queen is a proven evangelistic leader, both in the local church and in the academic setting, and I believe this book will be used by God to encourage pastors and church members to renew focus on the supreme task of winning souls to Christ."

—*Brandon Kiesling, associate pastor of young adults, First Baptist Church O'Fallon, Missouri*

"Are you ready to unleash your church to evangelize? *Mobilize to Evangelize* is a great tool for any church or church plant to get your church on the go to tell others about Jesus. Dr. Queen gives simple assessment tools for your church family to reach your entire community with the Good News of Jesus Christ. Every pastor and church planter should find a way to implement *Mobilize to Evangelize* into his evangelism and discipleship training."

—*Josh Crisp, pastor/NAMB church planter, Gospel Grove Church, Bargersville, Indiana*

"As the pastor goes, the people go. Brother pastors, if we want to see our people mobilized for evangelism, it starts with us, and Dr. Matt Queen issues a concise and actionable plan for you to lead in actively participating in evangelizing the lost, with the whole church in tow. Filled to the brim with Scripture and steps highlighted by helpful quotes, Dr. Queen does a masterful job bringing everything together to help you and your church go with Christ after the lost. I consider it not just an honor to endorse this book, but a duty, as this is a clarion call we must all heed."

—*Matt Henslee, pastor, Mayhill Baptist Church, Mayhill, New Mexico*

MOBILIZE

═══ TO ═══

EVANGELIZE

The Pastor and Effective
Congregational Evangelism

by
Matt Queen

Foreword by Nathan Lino

SEMINARY HILL
═══ PRESS ═══

Table of Contents

Foreword
By Nathan Lino

In my personal experience as a pastor, the greatest challenge of the responsibility to "do the work of an evangelist" is generating evangelistic momentum in a stagnant congregation; once momentum is lost, it is incredibly difficult to regain. I've learned the hard way that scolding, guilt, and shaming a congregation are ineffective catalysts to evangelism. I've also experienced the frustration of preaching sermons I was convinced would inspire an army of fervent missionaries only to watch the messages fall on mostly deaf ears. So, how does one get a stalled-out Great Commission vehicle moving again? You may be facing this challenge currently.

Seemingly, in every generation of the church, the Lord raises up a handful of lead evangelists with a special anointing to mobilize churches for evangelism. Matt Queen is one such man for our generation of the church. My relationship with Matt predates his holding of any educational degrees and formal leadership positions, and I can attest that he was an earnest and effective personal evangelist long before he had any official portfolio. I have also personally witnessed in him a 20-year track record of humility, prayerfulness, sincerity, abiding joy, and unconditional love and grace toward all people—characteristics that are only possible with an unusual grace gifting from the Holy Spirit. Additionally, I have seen many occasions on which Matt transformed apathetic Christians and local congregations, including mine, into excited soul-winners.

From small rural churches to large churches in growing cities, Matt has mobilized thousands of disciples to live on mission. Matt has a special anointing from God, and I commend him to you without hesitation as a leader you can trust to help you mobilize your church for evangelism.

You hold in your hands a highly practical tool that Matt has designed for this purpose. What follows is a step-by-step guide to leading a congregation through a healthy process that will clearly expose to them the need for evangelism, design a solution that fits your particular congregation, and launch its implementation. Two aspects of this tool I especially appreciate are that it is principle-based and thus flexible to any context, and that Matt anticipates our questions and concerns along the way and provides very helpful answers.

I have a hunch that you are going to keep this book on your desk, not your bookshelf.

Nathan Lino
Lead Pastor
Northeast Houston Baptist Church
Houston, Texas

Preface

Have you ever felt overwhelmed with your responsibility to lead God's people to be consistently and intentionally evangelistic? If so, I can relate. Dr. Paige Patterson, president of Southwestern Baptist Theological Seminary, hired me as an evangelism professor in 2010. On the evening of July 31, I received a phone call from him telling me that he wanted to see me the next day, my first day on the job, to discuss how the other evangelism professor, Dr. David Mills, and I were going to set the campus on fire for evangelism.

When our call ended, I looked to my wife and said, "Hope, tomorrow's my first and last day working at Southwestern Seminary." She asked, "Why do you say that, Matt?" I responded, "Because Dr. Patterson wants me to tell him how I am going to help lead Southwestern to be intentional and consistent in evangelism, and I don't know what I am going to tell him. What am I going to do?" I not only felt overwhelmed with such a responsibility; I felt like a failure before I had even begun.

With confidence and consolation, Hope replied, "Matt, tell him that with God's help you are going to do at Southwestern in evangelism what God has done through you at every church you've served." "What is that?" I asked. She said, "Just as you have done before, you will evangelize and equip others in evangelism by the power of the Holy Spirit and according to biblical principles. You will teach willing students, staff, faculty, and administrators at the seminary how to evangelize biblically in the power of the Spirit; then you will equip them to teach other willing students, staff, faculty, and administrators how to practice Spirit-empowered, biblically informed evangelism." All of a sudden, the stress and fear that overwhelmed me gave way to the peace of God.

Thanks be to God, He has set Southwestern Seminary on fire for evangelism! In fact, not only are students, staff, faculty, and administrators evangelizing every day, but since the 2013 fall semester, God has graciously saved at least one person every week during our fall and spring semesters. The key for me to lead Southwestern to evangelize intentionally and consistently lay in God's power and Word. He makes His power and Word available to you too, pastor, in order that you may *mobilize* your congregation to *evangelize!*

Matt Queen
L.R. Scarborough Chair of Evangelism ("The Chair of Fire")
Associate Professor of Evangelism
Southwestern Baptist Theological Seminary
Fort Worth, Texas

Introduction

Outside the work and power of the Holy Spirit, a church's pastor is the most influential factor upon its effectiveness in evangelism. No church will exceed its pastor's passion for and practice of evangelism. Likewise, no church will succeed in evangelism if its pastor fails to practice and have passion for evangelism. Thom Rainer's *Effective Evangelistic Churches* verifies the essential role of the pastor in a church's evangelistic effectiveness. His extensive research among evangelistically growing Southern Baptist churches determined, "Effective evangelism, humanly speaking, is the result of leadership. And the attitude of the leadership is perhaps one of the most critical factors in the growth of the church."[1]

Evangelism researchers and scholars from the 20th century until today have agreed on the overwhelmingly influential role of pastors upon the evangelistic effectiveness of their churches. As early as 1949, Faris Daniel Whitesell stated, "The [pastor], then, is the key-man in local church evangelism. The pastor must lead his people in intercessory prayer for the lost; he must inspire them, teach them, organize them, send them out, and encourage them to continue in this greatest of all church work."[2] Two decades later, in the 1970s, Eugene Skelton concluded from his study of the fastest growing Southern Baptist churches that, "A factor in the growth of these churches, and a fairly consistent one, is the

---

[1] Thom Rainer, *Effective Evangelistic Churches* (Nashville: Broadman, 1996), 195-196. Regarding "the attitude of the leadership," Rainer explains that these evangelistic pastors did the following: 1) believed in a supernatural God who is still working in His churches today; 2) communicated and modeled sincere love; 3) expressed themselves with happiness; and 4) exercised enthusiasm and energy.
[2] Faris Daniel Whitesell, *Basic New Testament Evangelism* (Grand Rapids: Zondervan, 1949), 144.

personal leadership of the pastor himself."[3] During that same time, Lewis A. Drummond asserted:

> [T]he pastor of a local congregation must assume the responsibility of leading and equipping the whole church to fulfill its ministry. It is to this position he has been called by the Holy Spirit. And regardless of how inadequate he may feel—or actually may be—to this work he must unreservedly give himself as best he can. … [T]he entire church becoming mobilized and equipped to evangelize our revolutionary society … settles essentially on the shoulders of the pastor.[4]

As late as 2008, a research report determined, "Evangelistic churches are led by evangelistic pastors … [who] operate from a deep sense of conviction. … The pastors of [effective and evangelistic Georgia churches took] responsibility for elevating evangelism through preaching, prayer, personal example, and purposeful strategies."[5]

Pastor, along with the primacy of the Holy Spirit's will and work, your example, expectations, and execution of congregational evangelism afford you everything you need in order to mobilize your church to evangelize! Lewis A. Drummond sounds a clarion call:

> The church is not going to be revolutionized inwardly so as to cope with the revolution outside until some forthright and courageous challenges are presented to it. And from what quarter will such a call and challenge

---

[3] Eugene Skelton, *Ten Fastest Growing Southern Baptist Sunday Schools* (Nashville: Broadman, 1975), 152.

[4] Lewis A. Drummond, *Leading Your Church in Evangelism* (Nashville: Broadman, 1975), 30.

[5] Steve R. Parr, Steve Foster, David Harrill, and Tom Crites, *Georgia's Top Evangelistic Churches: Ten Lessons from the Most Effective Churches* (Duluth: Georgia Baptist Convention, 2008), 7.

come? It seems self-evident from what quarter it should come, namely, the pastor. It is most important for the informed layman as well as for the ministry of the congregation to see that in a theology of church-centered evangelism, the pastor has the key role.[6]

Mobilize to Evangelize will assist you in understanding what you and your church think about evangelism; how you and your church practice evangelism; what is the perception among your staff and/or lay leaders, as well as your congregation, about evangelism; and what are some steps you can take as a pastor to mobilize your church to be effective in its evangelism. Though not a comprehensive solution to every church's evangelistic deficiencies, the book does suggest some solutions to many of the most common evangelistic weaknesses in a church. The first part of the book includes four questionnaires that will help you discern the state of evangelism in your congregation. The second part will help you interpret the results of the questionnaires and suggest some tangible next steps for the evangelistic mobilization of your church.

---

[6]Drummond, *Leading Your Church in Evangelism*, 25.

Part One

Four *Mobilize to Evangelize*
Assessment Questionnaires

As you consider what actions should be implemented in order to mobilize your congregation to evangelize, assessing yourself, your staff and/or lay leaders, and your members, as well as your church's recent trends, can assist you. This section provides four assessment questionnaires that identify the current trends, practices, philosophies, and perceptions of evangelism in your church.[7] These questionnaires include the following:

1. The *Annual Church Profile Questionnaire* should be completed by either the church's pastor, administrator, or secretary.

2. The *Pastor Assessment Questionnaire* should be completed by the pastor of the church.

3. The *Ministry Staff/Lay Leader Assessment Questionnaire* should be completed by every ministry staff member of the church. If the church does not employ ministry staff members beyond the pastor, the pastor should select lay leaders in the congregation to complete the questionnaire.

4. The *Church Member Assessment Questionnaire* ideally should be completed by all church members; however, some circumstances may warrant that it be completed by members of the church that the pastor selects.

Not every member of your staff/lay leadership and your congregation is required to complete an assessment questionnaire; however, the more people who complete an assessment

---

[7]These assessment questionnaires originated from survey questions posed by David Mills as a student assignment in his Contemporary Evangelism classes at Southwestern Seminary. I have modified and added to them.

questionnaire, the better you can understand your church's evangelistic realities and perceptions.

1. Annual Church Profile Questionnaire

Instructions: The Southern Baptist Convention (SBC) requests that each member church voluntarily submit an annual report of its statistical data, giving statement, and leadership profiles to its local Baptist associations and/or its state convention through the SBC Workspace database (formerly SBDS—Southern Baptist Directory Service).[8] If your church voluntarily submits this information to the convention, the *Annual Church Profile Questionnaire* will be a simple, fast, and accurate process. If your church either does not submit this information or is not affiliated with the SBC, the first questionnaire may take a little more time to research, but the time will be well spent. Based on your recent Annual Church Profile submissions or on data you have available or have researched, complete the requested information over the last five years for each of the following questions.

1. How many ***total church members*** did your church annually report over the last five years?

Year	Total Members Reported

---

[8]Voluntarily reporting SBC churches submit their Annual Church Profiles to their local Baptist associations and/or Baptist state conventions via paper forms or electronically through www.sbcworkspace.com. Roger S. Oldham offers a helpful, concise history of and reasoning for the use and reporting of Annual Church Profiles in "Annual Church Profile Gives Church, SBC 'Report Cards'"; accessed March 13, 2018; https://brnow.org/News/July-2014/Annual-Church-Profile-gives-churches-SBC-report-ca.

2. How many *total baptisms* did your church annually report over the last five years?

Year	Total Baptisms Reported

3. What is your church's annual *ratio of baptisms-to-total members* over the last five years? In other words, what is the ratio number of members your church reported for every one baptism your church reported?

Year	Baptisms-to-Total Members Ratio
	1 Baptism: _____ Total Members
	1 Baptism: _____ Total Members
	1 Baptism: _____ Total Members
	1 Baptism: _____ Total Members
	1 Baptism: _____ Total Members

4. What was the *total amount of undesignated and designated receipts* your church received and reported annually over the last five years?

Year	Total Receipts
	$
	$
	$
	$
	$

5. How many *dollars for intentional evangelism and/or missions expenditures* did your church annually report over the last five years?[9]

Year	Total Evangelism/Missions Expenditures
	$
	$
	$
	$
	$

6. What is your church's annual *ratio of intentional evangelism/ missions expenditures-to-total receipts* over the last five years? In other words, what is the ratio number of dollars spent on evangelism/missions expenditures to the total number of undesignated and designated receipts reported?

Year	Evangelism/Missions Expenditures-to-Total Receipts Ratio
	$1 Evangelism/Missions Expenditure: $ _____ Total Receipts
	$1 Evangelism/Missions Expenditure: $ _____ Total Receipts
	$1 Evangelism/Missions Expenditure: $ _____ Total Receipts
	$1 Evangelism/Missions Expenditure: $ _____ Total Receipts
	$1 Evangelism/Missions Expenditure: $ _____ Total Receipts

[9]Examples of intentional evangelism and/or missions expenditures can include but are not limited to funding the employment of an evangelism/missions staff member, mission trips, evangelism tracts, intentional evangelistic events, missions offerings, etc.

2. Pastor Assessment Questionnaire

Instructions: The *Pastor Assessment Questionnaire* asks you to answer two types of questions. First, you will be presented several groups of statements and asked to designate which of the statements in each group you affirm. Second, you will be asked to write your responses either to a single question or to a brief number of questions. If a question includes multiple inquiries, please respond to each of them.

1. Which of the following statements do you affirm?
(Check only the statements that apply):

☐ The Bible is inerrant in every area of reality (e.g., theology, history, science, etc.).

☐ The Bible's message is true, but it contains some historical and scientific errors.

☐ The Bible is a good book, but it is no more inspired than other great books.

———————————

☐ To be made right with God and go to heaven, people must repent of their sins and place their faith solely in Jesus Christ.

☐ Some people who do not personally know Jesus Christ as Savior and Lord will be in heaven.

☐ All persons will ultimately be saved.

☐ A real place of eternal, conscious torment awaits those who do not turn to Christ in this life.

☐ Unbelievers enter hell, but they are annihilated (i.e., they do not suffer eternal, conscious torment).

_____

☐ Every believer in Jesus Christ is responsible to evangelize.

☐ Only pastors, ministers, and evangelists should evangelize.

☐ Only grace-gifted evangelists, or those who appear to be good at evangelism, should evangelize.

_____

☐ Success in evangelism is doing evangelism.

☐ Success in evangelism is when an unbeliever becomes a believer.

_____

☐ When preaching and teaching in the presence of unbelievers, a pastor/teacher should always invite his hearers to repent of their sins, believe in Jesus Christ alone, and verbally confess, "Jesus is Lord."

☐ When preaching and teaching in the presence of unbelievers, a pastor/teacher should only in particular circumstances invite his hearers to repent of their sins, believe in Jesus Christ alone, and verbally confess, "Jesus is Lord."

☐ When preaching and teaching in the presence of unbelievers, a pastor/teacher should not invite his hearers to repent of their sins, believe in Jesus Christ alone, and verbally confess, "Jesus is Lord."

☐ My weekly duty to preach does not absolve me from also having a weekly responsibility to practice personal evangelism.

☐ My weekly duty to preach absolves me from having to practice personal evangelism weekly.

———————————

☐ Evangelism is that Spirit-empowered activity in which disciples of Jesus Christ give an intentional, verbal, and complete witness to His life, death, burial, and resurrection and invite unbelievers to become His disciples by repenting of their sins, believing in Christ alone, and verbally confessing, "Jesus is Lord."

☐ Evangelism is anything the church does, not always requiring the verbal sharing of the Gospel.

☐ Working for political, social, and/or environmental justice is just as important as verbally sharing the Gospel with those who do not believe in Jesus Christ.

☐ Working for political, social, and/or environmental justice is more important than verbally sharing the Gospel with those who do not believe in Jesus Christ.

———————————

☐ I have no problem looking people in the eyes, telling them, "Jesus loves you," and genuinely inviting them to repent and believe in Christ.

☐ I have no problem looking people in the eyes, telling them, "Jesus loves some sinners," and instructing only someone who is visibly under conviction of the Holy Spirit to repent and believe in Christ.

☐ I have no problem looking people in the eyes, telling them, "Jesus loves some sinners," and then trusting that the Holy

Spirit will regenerate them apart from my either inviting or instructing them to repent and believe in Christ.

☐ These are dark days, and I wonder if the Holy Spirit is working on unbelievers to turn them to Christ.

☐ This is a great day because I am certain the Holy Spirit works tirelessly and constantly to bring unbelievers to faith in Jesus Christ.

---

2. What do you understand to be the essential components of the Gospel message?

_____

_____

_____

3. How do you define evangelism?

_____

_____

_____

4. Do you consider yourself a consistent and intentional personal evangelist? If so, how do you practice personal evangelism, and in what way do you prefer to evangelize (e.g., intentional evangelism through relationships, visitation evangelism, social media, etc.)? If not, what is the most difficult obstacle preventing you from being a consistent and intentional personal evangelist?

_____

_____

_____

5. Do you ensure that your church's members are regularly trained/equipped in personal evangelism? If so, how often does this training/equipping occur?

_____

_____

_____

6. How are you and your members regularly equipped in personal evangelism training (e.g., what program(s), organization(s), book(s), or speaker(s) are used for evangelism equipping and training)? Specifically, what are you and your members trained to do in terms of personal evangelism (e.g., pray for unbelievers, make friends, make visits, share the Gospel, fold new believers into the church, etc.)?

_____

_____

_____

7. What specific expectations (either set by yourself or by the church), if any, do you have to ensure that you practice personal evangelism weekly? What specific expectations, if any, do you have of your staff members or lay leadership in terms of their commitment to practice personal evangelism weekly? What specific expectations, if any, do you have of your church members

in terms of their commitment to practice personal evangelism weekly?

> *Pastor:*
>
>
> *Staff Members or Lay Leadership:*
>
>
> *Church Members:*

8. If you have such expectations of yourself, your staff/lay leaders, and your congregation, how do you communicate and then measure them?

_____

_____

_____

9. Does your church conduct a weekly visitation ministry in which it seeks to reach guests and witness to unbelievers? If not, does it have some other intentional method of contacting guests and unbelievers?

_____

_____

_____

10. Does your church utilize evangelistic events to reach your community (e.g., Revivals, Vacation Bible School, Wild Game Banquets, Block Parties, Backyard Bible Clubs, etc.)? If so, how often do you offer these events, and in what ways does the church make these events intentionally evangelistic?

_____

_____

_____

11. How does the church "follow up" with new believers to lead them to become new members of your church and faithful disciples of Jesus Christ? Does the church require any training/class(es) before new believers are baptized and/or new members join your church?

_____

_____

_____

12. Do you encourage your church's members to make lists of unbelievers for whom they pray for salvation? If so, in what specific ways do you encourage them to do so?

_____

_____

_____

13. What is your understanding of the grace gift of the evangelist referenced in Ephesians 4:7-13 and the work of the evangelist in 2 Timothy 4:5-8? Are you a grace-gifted evangelist?

_____

_____

_____

14. Who in your church is a grace-gifted evangelist? How do you identify a grace-gifted evangelist in your congregation? How are these grace-gifted evangelists utilized in your church?

_____

_____

_____

15. Do you regularly identify and encourage those who consistently evangelize? If so, in what ways do you encourage them (e.g., send a note of encouragement, tell their stories to others, go evangelizing with them, etc.)?

_____

_____

_____

16. How do you describe your preaching (i.e., text-driven, expository, topical, or textual)?

_____

_____

_____

17. How often do you present the complete Gospel in your Sunday morning sermons (i.e., weekly, monthly, quarterly, annually, or only when the text warrants it)?

_____

_____

_____

18. Do you offer some form of a public invitation during your sermons? If so, what type(s) (e.g., prayer in the pew, altar call, decision room, raised hand, completion of a card, text message, etc.)? If not, why not?

_____

_____

_____

19. If you offer some form of a public invitation, how much time each week do you dedicate to the public invitation in your sermon preparation?

_____

_____

_____

20. Do any elements of your worship services contribute to evangelism? If so, what are these elements specifically?

_____

_____

_____

21. Do Sunday School/Small Group Bible Study classes practice open enrollment? That is, do they enroll people into the group at any place and at any time as long as the person agrees to be enrolled?

_____

_____

_____

22. Do you expect Sunday School/Small Group Bible Study teachers to explain the Gospel in each lesson? If so, how do you communicate and then measure this expectation?

_____

_____

_____

23. In what specific ways does your church evangelize those under the age of 18?

_____

_____

_____

24. In what areas do you believe your church is strong in evangelism?

_____

_____

_____

25. What do you believe your church needs to do to improve its evangelism effectiveness? Specifically, what do you believe you need to do in order to improve your church's evangelistic effectiveness?

Church's Action(s):

Pastor's Action(s):

3. Ministry Staff/Lay Leader Assessment Questionnaire

Instructions: The *Ministry Staff/Lay Leader Assessment Questionnaire* asks you to answer two types of questions. First, you will be presented several groups of statements and asked to designate which of the statements in each group you affirm. Second, you will be asked to write your responses either to a single question or to a small number of questions. If a question includes multiple inquiries, please respond to each of them.

1. Which of the following statements do you affirm?
(Check only the statements that apply):

☒ The Bible is inerrant in every area of reality (e.g., theology, history, science, etc.).

☐ The Bible's message is true, but it contains some historical and scientific errors.

☐ The Bible is a good book, but it is no more inspired than other great books.

_____

☒ To be made right with God and go to heaven, people must repent of their sins and place their faith solely in Jesus Christ.

☐ Some people who do not personally know Jesus Christ as Savior and Lord will be in heaven.

☐ All persons will ultimately be saved.

☒ A real place of eternal, conscious torment awaits those who do not turn to Christ in this life.

☐ Unbelievers enter hell, but they are annihilated (i.e., they do not suffer eternal, conscious torment).

_____

☒ Every believer in Jesus Christ is responsible to evangelize.

☐ Only pastors, ministers, and evangelists should evangelize.

☐ Only grace-gifted evangelists, or those who appear to be good at evangelism, should evangelize.

_____

☒ Success in evangelism is doing evangelism.

☒ Success in evangelism is when an unbeliever becomes a believer.

_____

☒ Evangelism is that Spirit-empowered activity in which disciples of Jesus Christ give an intentional, verbal, and complete witness to His life, death, burial, and resurrection and invite unbelievers to become His disciples by repenting of their sins, believing in Christ alone, and verbally confessing, "Jesus is Lord."

☐ Evangelism is anything the church does, not always requiring the verbal sharing of the Gospel.

☐ Working for political, social, and/or environmental justice is just as important as verbally sharing the Gospel with those who do not believe in Jesus Christ.

☐ Working for political, social, and/or environmental justice is more important than verbally sharing the Gospel with those who do not believe in Jesus Christ.

☒ Christians can know truth.

☐ Christians who claim to know the truth are arrogant. All we can hope to have and know are opinions.

☐ These are dark days, and I wonder if the Holy Spirit is working on unbelievers to turn them to Christ.

☒ This is a great day because I am certain the Holy Spirit works tirelessly and constantly to bring unbelievers to faith in Jesus Christ.

---

2. What do you understand to be the essential components of the Gospel message?

I Corinthians 15 : Life death and resurrection
Romans 3/6 : All sin. All can receive gift of salv.
Romans 10 : Repent, confess, and believe

3. How do you define evangelism?

A testimony of Jesus' life, death, and resurrection to the lost. An appeal to them to repent and believe for forgiveness and new life in discipleship.

4. Do you consider yourself a consistent and intentional personal evangelist? If so, how do you practice personal evangelism, and in what way do you prefer to evangelize (e.g., intentional evangelism through relationships, visitation evangelism, social media, etc.)? If

31

not, what is the most difficult obstacle preventing you from being a consistent and intentional personal evangelist?

I think perspective and planning (also prayer)

5. Does your pastor expect you to evangelize every week? If so, what specific expectations does he communicate, and how does he communicate them?

Yes, in contract. No, in statement.

6. Does your pastor expect the congregation to evangelize every week? If so, what specific expectations does he communicate, and how does he communicate them?

Yes, but no direct expectations. Communicates desire for ev. at beg. and end of worship.

7. In what specific ways do you encourage the practice of evangelism in your area of ministry/leadership?

EV training, white boarding, discipleship.

8. What one thing could your pastor do that would increase your motivation to evangelize?

Celebrate evangelism, encourage, organize, train (this class)

9. Do you regularly identify and encourage those who consistently evangelize? If so, in what ways do you encourage them (e.g., send a note of encouragement, tell their stories to others, go evangelizing with them, etc.)?

No.

10. In what areas do you believe your church is strong in evangelism?

Strong in personal invitations to join us for worship.

11. What do you believe your church needs to do to improve its evangelism effectiveness? Specifically, what do you believe you need to do in order to improve your church's evangelistic effectiveness?

Church's Action(s):

I need to continue to encourage and celebrate students who d.

Pastor's Action(s):

Same M

12. Do you regularly pray for the salvation of unbelievers? If so, for whose salvation are you currently praying?

Yes. Ben Savage and Jake Harris.
Keshay Tygr.

4. Church Member
Assessment Questionnaire

Instructions: The *Church Member Assessment Questionnaire* asks you to answer two types of questions. First, you will be presented several groups of statements and asked to designate which of the statements in each group you affirm. Second, you will be asked to write your responses either to a single question or to a small number of questions. If a question includes multiple inquiries, please respond to each of them.

1. Which of the following statements do you affirm? *(Check only the statements that apply):*

☐ The Bible is inerrant in every area of reality (e.g., theology, history, science, etc.).

☐ The Bible's message is true, but it contains some historical and scientific errors.

☐ The Bible is a good book, but it is no more inspired than other great books.

―――――――

☐ To be made right with God and go to heaven, people must repent of their sins and place their faith solely in Jesus Christ.

☐ Some people who do not personally know Jesus Christ as Savior and Lord will be in heaven.

☐ All persons will ultimately be saved.

―――――――

☐ A real place of eternal, conscious torment awaits those who do not turn to Christ in this life.

☐ Unbelievers enter hell, but they are annihilated (i.e., they do not suffer eternal, conscious torment).

_____

☐ Every believer in Jesus Christ is responsible to evangelize.

☐ Only pastors, ministers, and evangelists should evangelize.

☐ Only grace-gifted evangelists, or those who appear to be good at evangelism, should evangelize.

_____

☐ Success in evangelism is doing evangelism.

☐ Success in evangelism is when an unbeliever becomes a believer.

_____

☐ Evangelism is that Spirit-empowered activity in which disciples of Jesus Christ give an intentional, verbal, and complete witness to His life, death, burial, and resurrection and invite unbelievers to become His disciples by repenting of their sins, believing in Christ alone, and verbally confessing, "Jesus is Lord."

☐ Evangelism is anything the church does, not always requiring the verbal sharing of the Gospel.

☐ Working for political, social, and/or environmental justice is just as important as verbally sharing the Gospel with those who do not believe in Jesus Christ.

☐ Working for political, social, and/or environmental justice is more important than verbally sharing the Gospel with those who do not believe in Jesus Christ.

☐ Christians can know truth.

☐ Christians who claim to know the truth are arrogant. All we can hope to have and know are opinions.

☐ These are dark days, and I wonder if the Holy Spirit is working on unbelievers to turn them to Christ.

☐ This is a great day because I am certain the Holy Spirit works tirelessly and constantly to bring unbelievers to faith in Jesus Christ.

---

2. What do you understand to be the essential components of the Gospel message?

_____

_____

_____

3. What is evangelism?

_____

_____

_____

4. Do you consider yourself to be someone who evangelizes? If so, how often do you evangelize? If not, what is the most difficult obstacle that has prevented you from evangelizing?

_____

_____

_____

5. Does your pastor expect you to evangelize every week? If so, what specific expectations does he communicate, and how does he communicate them?

_____

_____

_____

6. Whom do you consider the most evangelistic person(s) in your church?

_____

_____

_____

7. Does anyone in your church consistently encourage and inspire you to evangelize? If so, who?

_____

_____

_____

8. What one thing could your pastor do that would increase your motivation to evangelize?

_____

_____

_____

9. Do you believe your church is strong in evangelism? If so, why? If not, why not?

_____

_____

_____

10. Do you regularly pray for the salvation of unbelievers? If so, for whose salvation are you currently praying?

_____

_____

_____

Part Two

Next Steps for Evangelistic Congregational Mobilization

Now that you and your church's trends, staff and/or lay leaders, and members have been assessed, you can begin processing the data you have collected to identify your next steps for evangelistic mobilization. Each survey question may be categorized according to nine structural components of congregational evangelism:

1. Disciple-Making and Evangelism
2. Evangelistic Funding
3. Evangelistic Theology
4. Philosophy of "Evangelism" and the "Work of the Evangelist"
5. Evangelistic Expectations
6. Evangelistic Practices
7. Evangelistic Preaching
8. Evangelistic Prayer
9. Evangelistic Training

Compare the answers on the questionnaires with each of the corresponding structural components that follow. Then utilize the *Strategic Actions* area to articulate the necessary adjustments and strategic actions you should take to mobilize your congregation for evangelistic effectiveness.

1. Disciple-Making and Evangelism

Refer to the responses to *Annual Church Profile Questionnaire* question 3 and *Pastor Assessment Questionnaire* questions 11, 21, 22, and 23 as you read and consider any strategic actions you need to plan and implement to improve your church's disciple-making and evangelism.

Baptism-to-Total Members Ratio

As of this book's publication, the latest published Annual Church Profile assessment data for churches of the Southern Baptist Convention took place in 2016. On July 8, 2017, LifeWay Christian Resources reported of that data: "The [collective] ratio of baptisms to total members [by all reporting churches] was one baptism for every 54 members."[10] Ideally this ratio would be low; however, the ratio of baptisms to total Southern Baptists has been on the rise for decades. The increase in this ratio means that insofar as information has been reported by Southern Baptist churches, more Southern Baptists account for fewer baptisms.

Consult your church's baptism-to-total members ratio in *Annual Church Profile Questionnaire* question 3. Ensure the ratio reflects those whom your church considers members, not merely the number of people who attend your Sunday morning worship service. Is your church's ratio higher or lower than the Southern Baptist number? Does the ratio surprise you? Would it surprise your congregation? What factors, emphases, or events may have contributed to your ratio being lower some years and higher others? In what ways could you lead your church to lower its ratio? Consider using the ratio and its five-year trend either to encourage your church in its evangelistic effectiveness (if applicable) or to begin the conversation with your church about how it might become more evangelistically effective (if applicable).

Evangelism with Disciple-Making in Mind

The desired result of biblical evangelism is not merely a decision; it is a baptized disciple who is taught to obey Christ and all His commands. Those who evangelize should assume that people who hear and believe the Gospel, in that moment, become disciples of Jesus Christ. However, personal evangelists should not assume new disciples instinctively know they should be baptized and should

---

[10] Carol Pipes, "Southern Baptists Report More Churches in 2016; Baptism, Membership Decline"; accessed March 13, 2018; https://blog.lifeway.com/news-room/2017/06/08/southern-baptists-report-more-churches-in-2016-baptisms-membership-decline/.

obey Christ's commands, or that some random church or person will ensure that new disciples are baptized and taught to obey all the commands of Christ. Unfortunately, many evangelizing believers make this assumption.

In fact, sometimes a personal evangelist unintentionally sounds like he either is utilizing a "bait and switch" technique in his evangelistic appeal or is prescribing a type of "works salvation" in his initial discipling instruction of a new Christian. Perhaps these unintended approaches constitute one of a number of reasons for recent baptism declines in the SBC. A prime example of these unintended perceptions occurs when the personal evangelist invites an unbeliever to receive Christ by saying something like, "All I'm asking you to do is call on the name of the Lord" (Romans 10:13). Then, immediately after he prays and asks God to forgive him, the personal evangelist tells him, "Now you must be baptized, read the Bible, pray to God every day, and put away any known sin." The new believer may either be thinking, "I thought he said all he was going to ask me to do was pray, and now there's a lot more he wants me to do"; or, "I thought I was forgiven of my sins when I asked God for it, but now it sounds like I have to do much more to be forgiven."

To avoid these inadvertent perceptions, you and your church members would be well-served to articulate the Gospel in such a way that naturally connects with the initial instruction you provide following a sinner's prayer confessing Jesus as Lord. Consider three natural evangelism-to-discipleship bridges found in the Gospel:

A. Include Christ's death, burial, and resurrection so you can naturally instruct a new disciple to be baptized.

Numerous Gospel presentations focus on Christ's death for sins to the exclusion of His burial and resurrection. The inclusion of all three events (cf., 1 Corinthians 15:3-4) affords you a direct connection between evangelism and discipleship. One such way includes telling the new believer:

A moment ago, I shared with you how Jesus died for your sins, was buried, and was raised from the dead. The Bible prescribes for you to profess your faith in what I have shared with you by presenting yourself for believer's baptism by immersion. When you are laid back into the water, you are professing you believe that Jesus died for your sins and was buried. Then, as you are lifted from the water, you are professing your belief in His resurrection from the dead.

B. Utilize Scripture so you can naturally instruct a new disciple to read the Bible.

Incorporating the previous Scriptures you paired with the essentials of your Gospel presentation assists you in advising a new believer to read the Bible. For example, tell him something like:

> Remember the Scriptures I shared with you that explained to you about who Jesus was and what He expects of you? God wants you to learn more about Him and His expectations for you now that you are His child. You will find this information in the Bible.

C. Invite your hearers to confess "Jesus is Lord" so you can naturally instruct a new disciple to pray and to put away any known sins.

Though under criticism of late, the use of a prayer to convey a sinner's contrition before God, as well as to confess verbally that Jesus is Lord, proves helpful in connecting evangelism and discipleship. Such a connection can be conveyed by explaining:

> Just a moment ago, you had your first conversation with God. The Bible refers to this conversation with God as "prayer." God wants you to continue to communicate with Him in this way. Also, you confessed to God in that prayer your belief that Jesus is Lord.

Additionally, what things are you now doing that you know you need to cease in order to submit to Jesus' rule and reign in your life? And what things are you not doing for Christ that you need to begin? In other words, what are some changes you need to make in order to demonstrate Jesus is your Lord?

Evangelistic Sunday Schools and/or Small Groups

Does your church utilize Sunday School and/or Small Groups? If not, you may be surprised to know that churches that have leveraged their Sunday Schools and/or Small Groups for evangelism have experienced evangelistic growth. If so, does your church consider or realize the evangelistic potential of its Sunday School and/or Small Groups?

In 2008, Georgia Baptist churches were asked, "Are your small groups/Sunday School classes intentionally connected to your outreach strategy?" The following chart displays the results:

Response	% Response	Average Baptisms	Worship Attendees to Baptism Ratio
No	41%	5.9	18.5 to 1
Yes	59%	14.5	15.9 to 1

They concluded, "The churches that make the connection baptized 16.3% more when viewing as a ratio and almost three times as many when viewing as a total. Similar studies have shown a connection between training and the growth of small groups and Sunday School."[11] How could your church benefit from using its Sunday School and/or Small Groups evangelistically?

Consider two simple ways as you discuss with God and the leaders in your church other means to utilize your Sunday School and/or Small Groups for evangelistic purposes. First, communicate

---

[11] Steve R. Parr and Thomas Crites, *Evangelistic Effectiveness: A Research Report* (Duluth: Baxter Press, 2012), 39.

an expectation to your Sunday School/Small Group Bible Study teachers that they explain the Gospel in each lesson they teach. Some unbelieving guests who visit these classes may feel more comfortable in a small group atmosphere than they do in a worship service to ask questions or respond to the Gospel. Brainstorm different ways you can communicate this expectation to your teachers and how you might reinforce it over time. If you have a minister of education and/or Sunday School director, employ his assistance in publicizing and measuring this expectation among your teachers.

Second, consider practicing *open enrollment* in your church's Sunday School and/or Small Groups, if you do not already. *Open enrollment* means that classes enroll people in the class at any place and at any time, so long as the person agrees to be enrolled. Numerous Sunday School and/or Small Group classes enroll people only after they have attended the class after a set number of times, and they will un-enroll people who have not attended after a certain number of times. Usually this type of enrollment places the onus on each enrolled member's commitment to the class.

Open enrollment shifts the responsibility to the class' commitment to enrolled members. Therefore, members of the class who attend seek to invite local family members, neighbors, friends, co-workers, and new acquaintances to join their class so it can exercise an obligation to these enrollees. Most of these newly enrolled members will be inactive in church, or de-churched altogether; thus, the class will seek to minister to them weekly by contacting them to pray for them and their requests, invite them to attend class and worship on Sunday, and ask them to attend social functions and fellowship events of the church. Enrolled members will not be removed from the roll unless they request to be removed or until the class makes a conscious decision no longer to care enough about them to reach them intently.

Disciple-Making among Those 18 and Under

Members of the 2017-18 presidentially appointed Southern Baptist Convention Evangelism Task Force were provided with Bill Day's unpublished research through New Orleans Baptist Theological Seminary's Leavell Center for Evangelism and Church Health. In it, Day reported:

> I chose the period from the year before the highest number of baptisms in the SBC [1971] to 2014. It is interesting that the group with the lowest baptisms in 1972 (adults) have now become the highest group. It is also interesting that while baptisms of children and youth were having their steepest decline (1971-75), young adults and adults were having a period of growth. However, from 1975 to 1978, all four groups experienced major decline. It is a great concern to me that the baptisms of young adults have declined from 102,260 in 1980 to 51,192 in 2014 (a 67.5% decrease), the baptisms of youth have declined from 137,667 in 1972 to 71,457 in 2014 (a 48.1% decrease), and children baptisms have declined from 159,770 in 1972 to 89,775 (a 43.8% decrease). Only adult baptisms have exceeded their 1972 total, going from 66,324 to 92,877 (a 40% increase).

Historically, Southern Baptists have reaped their greatest evangelistic harvest among children and teenagers, but this trend is alarmingly decreasing. To be sure, some of these childhood and adolescent decisions have proven later to have been premature; however, many others of these decisions appear to have been genuine. In order to guard against premature decisions, pastors, ministry staff members, teachers, and parents should carefully and intently ensure their children do not make a decision to receive Christ before such a time that they can both comprehend the Gospel and exhibit the Holy Spirit is convicting them of their sins. Nevertheless, these church leaders must teach the Gospel to their children at the earliest possible age, encourage their children and teens to anticipate the Spirit's conviction of their sins in His time, and make themselves available to lead their children and teenagers to Christ upon demonstrating they understand the Gospel and are convicted by the Spirit.

What are some ways that you and your church could be more intentionally attentive to reaching your children and teenagers evangelistically? Consider what God might do if the Sunday School/Small Group classes in your churches were to hear and endeavor to follow the riveting example of C.E. Matthews, one of Southern Baptists' most effective evangelism leaders. Chuck Kelley recounts:

> C.E. Matthews always dreamed of making a name for himself as a major league baseball player. He did make a mark in history, but in an entirely different field. When an injury dashed his dream of athletic success, Matthews focused on success as an accountant. He was a rising star in his company when he was born again, a convert of the visitation program of a Baptist church near his home. He immediately became involved in church and was soon a leader in the Sunday School program.
>
> Matthews taught a class for boys in the youth department. On his way to work one morning, he noticed the headline story in the paper was about the death of a boy struck by lightning. When he looked at the picture he saw that the boy['s name] was Grady, a member of his class. He met the boy's father for the first time at the funeral. As they talked, the men realized that neither one of them knew whether or not Grady was a Christian. Matthews realized that he had been more concerned with teaching the class than leading his boys to Jesus. The tragedy marked a turning point for the future evangelism secretary [of the Home Mission Board]. By the end of the day, he spoke to each boy on his roll about salvation.

The urgency and passion for evangelism awakened by his inattention to the salvation of a boy he taught for months never left him.[12]

What changes do you need to lead your church to make in terms of disciple-making and evangelism? Write in the **DISCIPLE-MAKING AND EVANGELISM STRATEGIC ACTIONS** workspace below any steps or plans you have after reading this section to decrease your church's baptism-to-total members ratio, as well as any steps or plans you have to increase your church's disciple-making through evangelism.

DISCIPLE-MAKING AND EVANGELISM STRATEGIC ACTIONS

---

[12]Chuck Kelley, *How Did They Do It: The Story of Southern Baptist Evangelism* (N.C.: Insight Press, 1993), 30-31.

2. Evangelistic Funding

Refer to the responses to *Annual Church Profile Questionnaire* questions 4, 5, and 6 as you read and consider any strategic actions you need to plan and implement to improve your church's evangelistic funding.

Evangelism/Missions Expenditures-to-Total Receipts Ratio

A popular old adage wisely says, "If you believe in something, then put your money where your mouth is." Do you and your church really believe evangelism and missions are necessary work in the Kingdom of God? If so, is this conviction reflected in your church's giving and spending toward evangelism/missions causes?

Refer back to the total giving patterns of your church in Annual Church Profile Questionnaire question 4. Then, review the pattern of how much your church has given in terms of evangelism/missions causes in Annual Church Profile Questionnaire question 5. Last, observe in Annual Church Profile Questionnaire question 6 the pattern of how many dollars your church spends on non-evangelism/missions expenditures to every one dollar expended on evangelism/missions causes.

Has your church's giving to evangelism/missions work increased, plateaued, or decreased over the past five years? Does the ratio of evangelism/missions expenditures to total receipts reflect what you believe to be a responsible stewardship of God's resources for Gospel work, or has your church failed in its investment of evangelism/missions causes? Are you surprised by the ratio? Would your congregation be surprised?

Write your answers to these questions in the **EVANGELISTIC FUNDING STRATEGIC ACTIONS** workspace. If changes in the church's financial support of evangelistic causes are warranted, record in the workspace any proposals that should be made to the group of people responsible for proposing your congregation's annual budget, as well as the staff members and lay leaders responsible for spending the resources of the annual budget, in order to improve your church's ratio of evangelism/ missions expenditures to total receipts.

Distinguishing between Evangelism and Marketing

Numerous corporations and individuals can testify of the success they have found in advertising, branding, and social media campaigns. Marketing can be successful for a church, as well. Church evangelism campaigns will benefit by the use of advertising dollars and attention. For example, advertisements in printed and digital outlets can be used in order to invite those who reside in your community to attend evangelistic events and services offered by your church. However, a temptation exists for a pastor and congregation either to convince themselves that advertising and evangelism are synonymous endeavors or to abandon the hours and effort of evangelism for dollars they can pay for advertisements. As I have written elsewhere:

> Pastors must not confuse evangelism with marketing. Numerous churches use advertising and/or branding in order to increase attendance at their services and events. Marketing can greatly assist churches in the work of their ministry in many ways. However, pastors may face the temptation to believe that marketing campaigns are the same as, if not a viable substitute for, evangelism. … Pastors should not feel guilty if they use marketing strategies for their churches, as long as they do not replace evangelism with marketing and continue to seek the lost through evangelism.[13]

How do you assess your church's use of advertising? Would advertising assist your church in its evangelistic events and endeavors? Do your church's ads/signs/publications promote its brand identity to the exclusion of the Gospel message? In the

---

[13] Matt Queen, "Seeking the Lost and Perishing," in *Pastoral Ministry: The Ministry of a Shepherd*, Deron Biles, ed. (Nashville: B&H Academic, 2018), 148-149.

workspace below, record any strategic action steps your church should take in regard to advertising for the purposes of evangelism.

EVANGELISTIC FUNDING
STRATEGIC ACTIONS

3. Evangelistic Theology

Refer to the responses to Pastor Assessment Questionnaire questions 1 (where applicable) and 2; Ministry Staff/Lay Leader Assessment Questionnaire questions 1 (where applicable) and 2; and *Church Member Assessment Questionnaire* questions 1 (where applicable) and 2 as you read and consider any strategic actions you need to plan and implement to improve your church's evangelistic theology.

Soteriological Convictions and Evangelism

Concerning theological convictions regarding salvation, the Gospel, and evangelism, Alvin Reid correctly states, "A conviction about a great salvation leads to a passion for evangelism."[14] However, even someone passionate for evangelism either can hold to erroneous theological convictions or alter his theological convictions over time. You and your church members' theological convictions concerning salvation inevitably contribute to the Gospel content you present to unbelievers. Therefore, your theological convictions and the Gospel message you proclaim must be tested continually by New Testament doctrine, instructions, and principles.

As the authoritative and foundational source for evangelism, the New Testament must inform the reasons for and the ways in which you and the members of your congregation evangelize. Would any of the responses you gave to questions in this category surprise your congregation? Were you surprised by any of the *Evangelistic Theology* responses submitted by your ministry staff/lay leadership or your congregation? Write any actions you and/or your staff need to take in order to correct any errant soteriological doctrine revealed by the questionnaire responses in the **EVANGELISTIC THEOLOGY STRATEGIC ACTIONS** workspace.

The Relationship between the Social Gospel and Evangelistic Decline

Review the *Evangelistic Theology* responses in question **1** of the *Pastor, Ministry Staff/Lay Leader*, and *Church Member Assessment Questionnaires* that deal with the praxes of *holism theology* and *prioritism theology*. In case these terms are new to you, David Hesselgrave provides succinct definitions of these theologically informed practices. He asserts that *holistic theology* advocates ministering to "society and individuals without dichotomizing between the physical and spiritual, or the body and the soul/spirit";

---

[14] Alvin Reid, *Evangelism Handbook: Biblical, Spiritual, Intentional, Missional* (Nashville: B&H, 2009), 141.

and he says *prioritism theology* primarily aims "to make disciples of all nations" while designating the nature of social justice causes and benevolence for physical needs as secondary and supportive.[15]

In their attempt to obey both the Great Commandment (Matthew 22:35-40) and the Great Commission (Matthew 28:19-20), Christians since the 20th century have experienced a ministry tension between the spiritual and the social, the soul and the body, the present age and the age to come, and ultimately orthodox and liberal theology. These tensions can affect churches in terms of either their growth or decline. C. Peter Wagner explains:

> Beginning with the Social Gospel Movement toward the end of the [19th] century, the mainline denominations embraced, to one degree or another, liberal theology. Liberal theology inevitably tends to dull the cutting edge of evangelism and church planting. At least one denominational study of membership decline indicated that their losses were not so much coming from current members who were deciding to leave the denomination, as from the failure of the churches to win new people to Christ and plant churches. At least three other studies, all done by mainline insiders, have shown a negative correlation of liberalism with membership growth and a positive correlation of theological conservatism.[16]

---

[15] David J. Hesselgrave, *Paradigms in Conflict* (Grand Rapids: Kregel, 2005), 122.

[16] C. Peter Wagner, *Leading Your Church to Growth* (Ventura: Regal, 1984), 33. The first study to which Wagner refers is Warren J. Hartman, *Membership Trends: A Study of the Decline and Growth in the United Methodist Church 1949-1975* (Nashville: Discipleship Resources, 1976). The latter three studies he references are: Dean Kelly, *Why Conservative Churches are Growing* (New York: Harper & Row, 1972); Dean R. Hoge, "A Test of Theories of Denominational Growth and Decline," and William J. McKinney, Jr., "Performance of United Church of Christ Congregations in Massachusetts and Pennsylvania," in *Understanding Church Growth and Decline 1950-1978*, Dean R. Hoge and David A. Roozen, eds. (New York: Pilgrim Press, 1979). More recent studies have verified the findings of these earlier studies, most notably Roger Fink and Rodney Stark, *The Churching of America, 1776-2005: Winners and Losers in Our Religious Economy*, rev. ed. (Piscataway: Rutgers University Press, 2005).

While you and your church members must demonstrate genuine concern for unbelievers, evangelism coupled with a social gospel theology has the potential to lead you to adopt some unwise evangelism philosophies and practices. For example, social gospelism usually convinces its advocates and practitioners that they must earn the right to evangelize a stranger. Attempting to earn the right to evangelize can foster a *quid pro quo* kind of evangelism, in which personal evangelists foster an expectation that those who receive their acts of service must listen to their Gospel presentations or feel guilty for not doing so. Over time, the path of social gospelism leads down a road of confusing benevolence with evangelism, or the promotion of an unhealthy interdependence between Gospel proclamation and mercy ministry. You and your members have an obligation to practice both Gospel proclamation and mercy ministry without the self-imposed guilt or expectation that you must do one in order to do the other.

Did any of the questionnaire responses uncover any concerns about how proclamation and action, or evangelism and ministry, operate in your church? If so, how will you lead your church to address these concerns? Note any correctives or action steps you plan to take in the **EVANGELISTIC THEOLOGY STRATEGIC ACTIONS** workspace.

EVANGELISTIC THEOLOGY
STRATEGIC ACTIONS

4. Philosophy of "Evangelism" and the "Work of an Evangelist"

Refer to the responses to Pastor Assessment Questionnaire questions 1 (where applicable), 3, 13, and 14; Ministry Staff/Lay Leader Assessment Questionnaire questions 1 (where applicable) and 3; and Church Member Assessment Questionnaire questions 1 (where applicable), 3, and 7 as you read and consider any strategic actions you need to plan and implement to improve your church's philosophy of "evangelism" and the "work of an evangelist."

Defining "Evangelism"

Lewis Drummond captured the tension between too broad and too narrow an understanding of "evangelism":

> ...[I]t is clear that the term *evangelism* is used by many today in too broad a sense and by others in too narrow a manner. For example, evangelism is simply not everything we do, as some seem to understand it. Although the spirit of evangelism should permeate all Christian activity and ministry, everything we do is not evangelism *per se*. It can be rather self-deceptive to define evangelism too broadly. It can even be a more subtle excuse for not engaging in outright, pointed evangelistic endeavors. Conversely, evangelism is surely more than just formally "preaching the Gospel." Communicating the good news is a much broader concept than doing no more than what the

preacher does from the pulpit. It clearly implies action as well as proclamation. And the entire church is to engage in it.[17]

Evangelism is that Spirit-empowered activity in which disciples of Jesus Christ give a complete and intentional witness to His life, death, burial, and resurrection, calling unbelievers to become His disciples by repenting of their sins, placing their faith in Christ alone, and verbally confessing, "Jesus is Lord." Biblical evangelism anticipates that those who hear and believe the Gospel immediately become disciples of Jesus Christ and must be baptized by a local church in the name of the Father, Son, and Spirit, as well as taught to obey all of Christ's commands.

Defining the "Work of an Evangelist"

G. Campbell Morgan presents his understanding that an evangelist's work, or function, is twofold:

> In the New Testament only two men are definitely spoken of as evangelists. Philip is called an evangelist, and in the final charge of Paul to Timothy, he says, "Fulfill thy ministry, do the work of an evangelist." It is at least significant that the two men who are called evangelists are in entirely different circumstances, and suggests as I think, the two types of the evangelist. Philip was a man at large. He was not definitely in charge of any Church, nor was he, as I believe, set apart by any apostolic function to his work. He was an evangelist, prepared by the impartation of a qualification for telling the Gospel, to tell the Gospel. He moves from place to place. He goes to Samaria, then he speaks to the individual eunuch, and is caught away to

---

[17]Drummond, *Leading Your Church in Evangelism*, 21-22. I would add that this "implied action" that accompanies "proclamation" includes making disciples of Jesus Christ, who both become members of a local church through believer's baptism in the name of the Father, Son, and Spirit and are taught obedience to all His commands.

Azotus. Then we find him moving up through Caesarea, at last settling down, his children coming up after him, and uttering the same great Gospel. That is an evangelist as I see him in the Acts of the Apostles.

The other man, who is in oversight of the Church at Ephesus, placed in oversight through certain difficulties arising there, and the letter of the apostle is written to instruct him in his work. I am inclined to think that the more special work of Timothy was that of the evangelist, moving from place to place. But Paul saw the necessity of a certain oversight at Ephesus, and sent him there. And he writes to him of his charge, the church; and instructs him as to how he shall take oversight; but the last thing the apostle urges is that he shall not forget that though he is now in oversight of the church through certain ecclesiastical difficulties, he is to fulfill his ministry, and do the work of an evangelist. It is at least significant that these two men are described by the term evangelist, the one moving from place to place, and the other settled in oversight of a church.[18]

Paul mentions the "work of an evangelist" in 2 Timothy 4:5. John R.W. Stott writes, "It is not clear whether the reference is to a specialist ministry such as is implied in the only other New Testament passages where the word occurs (Acts 21:8; Eph. 4:11). The alternative is to interpret it of anybody who preaches the Gospel and witnesses to Christ."[19] Jonathan Baldwin rightly explains: "2 Timothy 4:1-15 provides an outline of Paul's expectations for Timothy's ministry," and reference is not just to anyone who preaches the Gospel and witnesses for Christ. He continues:

---

[18] G. Campbell Morgan, *Evangelism* (East Northfield: The Bookstore, 1904), 53-54.
[19] John R.W. Stott, *Guard the Gospel: The Message of 2 Timothy* (Downers Grove: InterVarsity Press, 1973), 112.

[T]hese … verses encompass four groups of commands, specifically charged to Timothy's ministry. Each group of commands precedes a γάρ clause, which explains the purpose of the commands. The first group of commands urges Timothy in his use of God's word (2 Tim 4:2). The γάρ clause, which follows, explains that Timothy's use of Scripture will function as a tool to refute false teaching (2 Tim 4:3-4). The second group of commands directs Timothy in the fulfillment of his ministry (2 Tim 4:5). The γάρ clause, which follows, reveals the anticipated arrival of Paul's death (2 Tim 4:6-8). The third group of commands in regards to Timothy's ministry calls Timothy to come to Paul (2 Tim 4:9), bring Mark (2 Tim 4:11), and bring the cloak, the books, and all the parchments (2 Tim 4:13). The following γάρ clause explains Paul's circumstances in view of his companions and his needs (2 Tim 4:10-13). In the final command, Paul warns Timothy of Alexander the coppersmith (2 Tim 4:14-15). The γάρ clause explains Alexander's opposition to Paul's message.[20]

The last two imperatives—"Make every effort to come to me soon … bring[ing with you] the cloak which I left at Troas with Carpus, and the books, especially the parchments" (v. 9) and "Be on guard against [Alexander the coppersmith]" (v. 15)—are only applicable to Timothy's situation in his own time and place. However, the first two imperatives—"preach the word; be ready in season and out of season; reprove, rebuke, exhort, with great patience and instruction" (v. 2) and "be sober in all things, endure hardship, do the work of an evangelist, fulfill your ministry" (v. 5)—while specifically applicable to Timothy, can also be used to apply to grace-gifted evangelists throughout history, inasmuch

---

[20]Jonathan Baldwin, "Who Can Do the Work? A Biblical Examination of the Work of an Evangelist in 2 Timothy 4:1-15" (Ph.D. Seminar Paper, Southwestern Baptist Theological Seminary, 2017), 6-7.

as they should preach the Gospel with readiness, correct those in the church who reject sound doctrine (vv. 2-3), and carry on the kinds of ministry functions Paul performed (vv. 5-8), including planting churches and encouraging believers to preach the Gospel.

Related to this discussion, a prevalent misnomer has arisen that affirms "evangelism" and the "work of an evangelist" are synonymous in meaning. In his day, G. Campbell Morgan articulated this now common misunderstanding when he said of the "work of the evangelist": "The work of the evangelist is the perfecting of the number of the Church by calling men into relationship with Christ";[21] and when attributed to an "evangelist" that: "The evangelist is a name signifying a man who tells the glad tidings always with a view to constraining the man who listens by the evangel, to that of which the evangel bears testimony."[22] Understandings like these teach that the "work of an evangelist" is simply synonymous with doing evangelism. Likely, this concept has developed into what is now referred to as a "gift of evangelism"—a special spiritual ability to communicate the Gospel to unbelievers beyond the normal activity of sharing the Gospel.

In a previous blogpost, I discussed why the interpretation of the "work of the evangelist" errs when understood as evangelism, or a "gift of evangelism."[23] Some believers convince themselves that only those who possess "the gift of evangelism," or the "evangelist," have a responsibility to evangelize. Other believers accept the responsibility to fulfill the Great Commission through evangelism but conceive that those not "gifted" in evangelism or as an evangelist can practice it more passively and occasionally than those who affirm possessing the "gift" of evangelism or being gifted as an evangelist.

The Bible never mentions "a gift of evangelism." However, Paul does identify grace-gifted "evangelists" (Ephesians 4:11),

---

[21] Morgan, *Evangelism*, 44.
[22] Ibid., 50.
[23] Matt Queen, "Evangelism is Not a Spiritual Gift," April 4, 2017; http://theologicalmatters.com/2017/04/04/do-some-believers-possess-a-spiritual-gift-of-evangelism-or-do-all-believers-receive-the-holy-spirit-in-order-to-evangelize/.

whom he explains equip all saints for ministry along with the grace-gifted apostles, prophets, pastors, and teachers (Ephesians 4:12-13). In the contemporary era, Christ continues to equip believers for ministry through evangelists, pastors, and teachers. As such, all believers are responsible to be equipped for ministry, which includes being equipped by grace-gifted evangelists to evangelize. Rather than describe a spiritual "gift of evangelism" bestowed upon a select few, Scripture presents evangelism as a spiritual discipline to be practiced by all believers intentionally and consistently. Furthermore, Scripture identifies evangelists as those who are gifted by the Spirit to equip, encourage, train, and teach the saints in evangelism for their perfecting in ministry.

What would it mean for Christ's evangelistic enterprise if such a "gift of evangelism," or the idea of evangelism as the "work of an evangelist," did exist? A number of problems would arise. Consider the following:

1. If evangelism were a spiritual gift, then additional spiritual gifts would exist outside those identified in the New Testament. The New Testament spiritual gift inventory can be found in Romans 12:4-8; 1 Corinthians 12:1-31; Ephesians 4:7, 11-13; and 1 Peter 4:10-11. The following constitutes the Bible's list of spiritual grace gifts: a word of wisdom, a word of knowledge, faith, healing, effecting of miracles, prophecy, distinguishing of spirits, speaking in tongues, interpreting tongues, administration, service, exhortation, giving, leadership, mercy, apostles, prophets, evangelists, pastors, and teachers. This list verifies, as mentioned earlier, that the Bible never references "a gift of evangelism." If the Holy Spirit does endow some believers with a "gift of evangelism," then it follows that additional grace gifts of the Spirit exist outside those provided in Scripture. How can the existence of additional spiritual gifts not mentioned in Scripture be verified? What prevents

someone else from asserting a "gift of reading the Bible" or a "gift of prayer" as a reason why he does not have the responsibility to read the Bible or pray either consistently or at all?

2. If an evangelist were simply one who evangelized the lost, then the beneficiaries of spiritual gifts would need to be reconsidered. The New Testament's inventory and explanation of spiritual grace gifts demonstrates that the purpose of every spiritual gift is to unite diversely gifted believers in the body of Christ (Romans 12:5); to benefit the common good of the body (1 Corinthians 12:7); to equip the saints for the work of ministry (Ephesians 4:12); and to serve one another (1 Peter 4:10). Generally speaking, all the spiritual gifts are given to serve the body of Christ, not unbelievers. Specifically, Ephesians 4 states that Christ gave evangelists to equip the saints, not to be the only ones who evangelize sinners. Rather than do the work of evangelism for the saints, grace-gifted evangelists equip and encourage the saints to do evangelism.

As you review the results from the questionnaires, do your staff/ lay leaders and church members articulate the same meaning of "evangelism" that you do? If not, how can you instruct them in a more biblical understanding of evangelism? Do you utilize either vocational or voluntary grace-gifted evangelists in the training, equipping, and encouraging of your members in evangelism? How can you utilize grace-gifted evangelists while still leading your church in evangelism? Write your answers in the **PHILOSOPHY OF "EVANGELISM" AND THE "WORK OF AN EVANGELIST" STRATEGIC ACTIONS** workspace.

PHILOSOPHY OF "EVANGELISM" AND THE "WORK OF AN EVANGELIST" STRATEGIC ACTIONS

5. Evangelistic Expectations

Refer to the responses to Pastor Assessment Questionnaire questions 1 (where applicable), 7, and 8; Ministry Staff/Lay Leader Assessment Questionnaire questions 1 (where applicable), 5, and 6; and *Church Member Assessment Questionnaire* questions 1 (where applicable) and 5 as you read and consider any strategic actions you need to plan and implement to improve your evangelistic expectations within the congregation.

Why the Pastor Must Set, Promote, and Measure Evangelistic Expectations

Outside the work of the Holy Spirit, a church's evangelistic success or failure is directly tied to its pastor's effectiveness in both setting and executing ministry expectations and goals. C.B. Hogue writes, "The most influential voice in the life of the church comes from the pulpit. Several times each week, the pastor has an opportunity to share his vision of the church and its mission. As the acknowledged leader ... the pastor can profoundly shape the ministry of his congregation. ... If he stresses growth, growth occurs."[24]

Congregations reflect their pastors. They value the things their pastors value. If the members of churches never see or hear of their pastors' evangelizing, their pastors will rarely, if ever, see or hear of it in their congregants. C.E. Autrey corroborates this claim:

> The place of the pastor in the evangelism of the local church is strategic. If he is evangelistic, the church will ordinarily be evangelistic. The degree to which the pastor is evangelistic will be reflected in the church. If he is lukewarm, the church will very likely be lukewarm. If he is intensely evangelistic, the church will reflect the warmth and concern of the pastor."[25]

Charles Roesel, retired pastor of First Baptist Church Leesburg, Florida, says, "People do not tend to drift toward evangelism, but drift away from it. Leaders must continually call the members back to evangelism."[26] If a pastor does not habitually communicate his weekly evangelistic expectations of himself, his staff, and his church, at best, his congregation and staff will assume that he does not have such expectations, and at worst, that he has not set any evangelistic expectations.

Do you have any specific evangelistic expectations of yourself, your staff/lay leaders, and your congregation? If so, have you ever articulated them on paper? Have you ever publicly articulated them from the pulpit? Pastors have articulated evangelistic

---

[24] C.B. Hogue, *I Want My Church to Grow* (Nashville: Broadman, 1977), 66.
[25] C.E. Autrey, *Basic Evangelism* (Grand Rapids: Zondervan, 1959), 63.
[26] Parr, Foster, Harrill, and Crites, *Georgia's Top Evangelistic Churches*, 7.

expectations to their congregations in a number of ways, including: (1) proposing for members a weekly number of intentional Gospel conversations they should aim to have; (2) expecting members to attend a weekly, monthly, or quarterly evangelistic event/outreach of the church; and (3) encouraging members to adopt what Charles Stewart refers to as "witnessing rules, or principles,"[27] to name a few. If you have not ever, or recently, articulated evangelistic expectations of yourself, your staff/lay leaders, or your congregation, consider what evangelistic expectations God desires for you to have and write them in the **EVANGELISTIC EXPECTATIONS STRATEGIC ACTIONS** workspace.

How the Pastor Can Set, Promote, and Measure Evangelistic Expectations

How can a pastor effectively articulate the evangelistic expectations he has of his congregation? For starters, he should not assume all his congregants are aware he has such expectations. Probably not everyone in a church knows them; and if his people do not know them, they are not likely to evangelize consistently.

A pastor whose church understands and meets his evangelistic expectations is one who frequently reiterates them and encourages the same of his staff and lay leadership. When a pastor believes his promotion of evangelism to be monotonous, his staff and/or lay leaders are just beginning to listen. When the staff/lay leaders join in the pastor's promotion to the point where they believe it has become monotonous, the congregation is just beginning to

---

[27] Charles Stewart is a former pastor in Georgia and Texas who currently serves as an adjunct professor of applied ministries at Southwestern Seminary. He has adopted and encouraged others to adopt the following "witnessing rules, or principles," as he calls them, to guide and encourage a personal practice of soul-winning: 1) *The Five-Minute Rule*: If I have a captive audience with another person for five minutes, I will try to engage them in a Gospel conversation; 2) *The Homestead Rule*: If someone comes onto my home property, I will seek to engage them in a Gospel conversation; and 3) *The Holy Spirit Rule*: If the Holy Spirit directs me to do so, I will seek to engage that person in a Gospel conversation. As he readily admits, these "rules" are intended to be guidelines to encourage evangelism, not legalistic so as to incur guilt.

listen. The more a pastor and his staff/lay leaders articulate the goal for every church member to evangelize, the more people actually hear it and the more the pastor can expect them to do it.

In addition to announcing his evangelistic goals among the congregation, a pastor must practice personal evangelism and be seen doing it in the community. Normally, consistent and intentional evangelism in a church does not begin with everyone at once; rather, it begins with the pastor investing in a few people with the aim of multiplying the process. Specifically, a pastor should find those in his congregation who are willing to go evangelizing with him in the community so that he can first train them how to evangelize. Once they learn, he can then teach them how to train other willing members of the church to evangelize in the same way he has trained them. In advising how a pastor should enlist his people to evangelize, C.H. Spurgeon explained his counsel:

> Sometimes, the very best plan would be to call all the members of the church together, tell them what you would like to see, and plead earnestly with them that each one should become for God a soul-winner. Say to them, "I do not want to be your pastor simply that I may preach to you; but I long to see souls saved, and to see those who are saved seeking to win others for the Lord Jesus Christ." … Then, if that should not succeed, God may lead you to *begin with one or two*.
>
> There is usually some "choice young man" in each congregation; and as you notice deeper spirituality in him than in the rest of the members, you might say to him, "Will you come down to my house on such-and-such an evening that we may have a little prayer together?" You can gradually increase the number to two or three godly young men if possible…. Having secured their sympathy, you might say to them, "Now we will try if we cannot influence the whole church; we will begin with our fellow-members before we go to the outsiders…."

… Your work, brethren, is to set your church on fire somehow. You may do it by speaking to the whole of the members, or you may do it by speaking to the few choice spirits, but you must do it somehow.[28]

A pastor should also seek to identify the members of his church who evangelize in order to promote evangelism within the congregation. Church members respond to their pastor's encouragement. Ask church members to keep you informed about their personal soul-winning activities. When they do, consider sharing a brief testimony from the pulpit of how members are actively sharing the Gospel, and/or send a brief note or email periodically to appreciate them for their faithful evangelism. In your staff meetings, include time for you and the staff to share about recent witnessing encounters, and encourage those whom you sense are struggling in the spiritual discipline of evangelism. When your staff meets, as well as during your quiet time, ensure you pray for the lost people whom your members are seeking to reach through evangelism. Brainstorm some of the ways you intend to promote evangelism and your evangelistic expectations of the congregation in the **EVANGELISTIC EXPECTATIONS STRATEGIC ACTIONS** workspace.

EVANGELISTIC EXPECTATIONS
STRATEGIC ACTIONS

---

[28] C.H. Spurgeon, *The Soul Winner* (London: Passmore & Alabaster, 1895), 99-100.

6. Evangelistic Practices

Refer to the responses to *Pastor Assessment Questionnaire* questions 4, 9, 10, 15, 20, 24, and 25; Ministry Staff/Lay Leader Assessment Questionnaire questions 4 and 7-11; and *Church Member Assessment Questionnaire* questions 4, 6, 8, and 9 as you read and consider any strategic actions you need to plan and implement to improve the evangelistic practices within your church.

The Pastor and His Evangelistic Practices

No pastor should do all the evangelism for his church, but he must both promote and encourage all the evangelism of his church. C.E. Autrey writes:

> There are some instances in which the pastor feels his evangelistic responsibility so keenly that he tries to do all the soul-winning [for his church]. This is an error. He must set the example and then lead the entire church membership to follow. ... A devastating heresy today is found in the belief that the pastor should do all the soul-winning while the church indulges in complacency.[29]

A pastor who desires to be a personal soul-winner must strive to schedule evangelism concurrently with the execution of his

---

[29] Autrey, *Basic Evangelism*, 63-64.

daily pastoral activities. Evangelism may not always take place when a pastor expects it, but it will never take place if he does not intentionally schedule it. He will find that failing to plan time to evangelize will result in failing to find time to evangelize.

Keep in mind that your routine will fluctuate in the frequency of your many pastoral duties, including your spiritual duty to evangelize. This phenomenon results from the daily, multiple tasks required of you (i.e., feeding the sheep, caring for the sick, and going after the scattered) constraining your schedule and making it genuinely difficult to fulfill all your duties. Oftentimes you will be tempted to relegate evangelism to the end of your to-do list, but resist this temptation! Other times, the overwhelming number and nature of your responsibilities will leave you discouraged or feeling overly exhausted. Few things cure pastoral discouragement and/or exhaustion like leaving the office in order to seek a sinner to evangelize. First, you realize that someone is in a worse condition than you; and second, the Gospel reminds you of God's abiding love for you.

Have you identified any changes you need to make in your schedule in order to be more evangelistically consistent? Note any changes you need to implement in the **EVANGELISTIC PRACTICES STRATEGIC ACTIONS** workspace.

The Church and Its Evangelism Strategies

In 2011, Steve Parr and Thomas Crites asked 2,081 Georgia Baptist churches to respond to the following statement: *We have an intentional evangelism strategy.* The results of the responses are found in this chart:

Response	% Response	Average Baptisms	Worship Attendees to Baptism Ratio
No	45%	5.8	18.8 to 1
Yes	55%	15.3	15.7 to 1

As illustrated by the chart, their research concluded:

> The key stat is the "Worship Attendees to Baptism Ratio" because it places churches of all sizes on equal footing in order to compare results. A higher ratio indicates that it takes more members to lead someone to faith in Christ, making the lower ratio preferable. Based on the ratios, the churches that have an intentional evangelism strategy baptize almost twenty percent (20%) more than those that do not. The difference increases to three times as many if looking exclusively at total baptisms.[30]

In another study, they asked Georgia Baptist pastors to list what they believed to be the top three most effective evangelistic strategies of their churches. They compared these perceived effective evangelistic strategies to the number of baptisms in the churches to measure to what extent these perceptions reflected reality. They explained their process when they wrote:

> For example, we took all of the churches that listed "mission trips" as one of their top three most effective evangelistic methods and then looked at the total baptisms for all of the churches that gave that response and divided the total by the worship average to get a baptism ratio. A lower ratio is indicative of greater effectiveness. Each of these strategies and methods can be used in seeing people come to faith in Jesus Christ. However, you may be surprised at the results:[31]

---

[30] Parr and Crites, *Evangelistic Effectiveness*, 30.
[31] Ibid., 44-45.

Rank	Method	Baptism Ratio	Perceived Rank
1	Door-to-door Evangelism	13.2	8
T2	Visitation	13.7	7
T2	Personal Witnessing	13.7	4
4	Outreach Events	14.9	5
5	Worship Service Invitation	15.0	3
6	Revival Services	15.4	6
7	Media & Printed Materials	15.5	11
8	Children & Youth Programs	16.1	2
9	VBS	16.8	1
10	Servant Evangelism	17.1	10
11	Mission Trips	18.9	9

Are you surprised by the results? Would the evangelistic perceptions and realities be similar in your church? Does your church have an intentional evangelism strategy, or do your church members consistently evangelize without one? Do any similarities exist between your response to the statement *My church has an intentional evangelism strategy*, your average baptisms, and your members-to-baptisms ratio? Would your people benefit from a church-wide strategy? If so, what strategy should your church adopt? Record your answers in the **EVANGELISTIC PRACTICES STRATEGIC ACTIONS** workspace.

EVANGELISTIC PRACTICES
STRATEGIC ACTIONS

7. Evangelistic Preaching

Refer to the responses to *Pastor Assessment Questionnaire* questions 1 (where applicable) and 17-19 as you read and consider any strategic actions you need to plan and implement concerning your evangelistic preaching.

How Often Should Your Sermons Include an Evangelistic Appeal?

Shane Pruitt offers at least three reasons why church members should expect their pastor to include the Gospel in every sermon:

A. Hopefully, there are non-Christians in the crowd.

Sadly, through the years of ministry, I have heard church members from all different kinds of churches say, "Our pastor is always asking us to invite lost people to come to church with us. However, when we do, he never shares the Gospel." As preachers, if we're expecting church members to bring lost people, they should expect us to clearly communicate how their lost guests can be found. If we take sharing the Gospel seriously every weekend, then our congregants will take seriously the task of inviting the lost to hear it.

B. You are training church members how to share the Gospel.

As a pastor, I often did what any other pastor would do: I encouraged church members to regularly share their faith with their lost friends, neighbors, and co-workers. That is the mission of the church—to be making disciples that make disciples. The doorway into discipleship is believing the Gospel message and surrendering to Jesus. We expect our congregation to share their faith, but we never teach them how to do it. Obviously, this isn't the only evangelism training we should be doing, but one of the ways people can learn how to clearly explain the Gospel is by hearing their pastor do it every week at some point in the sermon. Each one of us can tend to be parrots at times. Meaning, we repeat what we hear over and over. If you want your members to repeat the Gospel, then let them hear it from you over and over and over again.

C. What we celebrate is what we are communicating as most important.

This is one of the simplest principles in any church, ministry, or even business. Whatever you celebrate is what you're telling people is most important to you. If your church mainly celebrates the budget and offering, then people will evaluate your success and failures based on the bottom dollar. As a leader, if you're mainly celebrating the worship attendance, then the congregation will be discipled into believing that is the measure of success— numbers up means God is blessing, numbers down must mean that God is not pleased and it may be time for a new pastor. However, communicating the Gospel and celebrating the lives that are being transformed by it every week is telling your congregation that this is the most important thing we could be doing. Not the results of the Gospel. That is up to the Lord. Celebrate faithfulness and obedience in proclaiming the Gospel. As the church, this is why we exist.[32]

Issuing a Public Invitation

Pastors should publicly invite unbelievers to repent, believe, and confess Jesus Christ as Lord without manipulating or pressuring them into what ultimately would be false decisions. As stated by Pruitt above, unbelievers attend virtually every venue where pastors preach. Because pastors cannot know the spiritual condition of everyone under the sound of their voices, they should include the Gospel and its appeal in every one of their sermons. "Public evangelistic invitations can take many forms, from pastors instructing unbelievers to come to them during services or after services, to completing and submitting information on a card for a subsequent meeting, to quietly exiting the sanctuary to spiritual counseling rooms."[33] Indicate in the **EVANGELISTIC PREACHING STRATEGIC ACTIONS** workspace what form(s) you find helpful to implement public invitations.

Pastors' sermons must include a call for decision for at least two reasons. First, the overwhelming majority of sermons recorded in the New Testament include a call for unbelievers to believe in Jesus Christ for salvation and to repent of their sins (e.g., Matthew 3:2; 4:17; Mark 1:14-15; Acts 2:38; 3:19; 14:15; 26:20). As Edward Rommen states, "Given the personal nature of the Gospel, evangelism is essentially the issuing of an invitation to participate in the restoration offered by Christ."[34]

---

[32] Shane Pruitt, "Awaiting Gospel Preaching: Should Church Members Expect the Gospel in Every Sermon?" April 11, 2018; http://preachingsource.com/blog/awaiting-Gospel-preaching-should-church-members-expect-the-Gospel-in-every-sermon/.

[33] Queen, "Seeking the Lost and Perishing," 151.

[34] Edward Rommen, *Get Real: On Evangelism in the Late Modern World* (Pasadena: William Carey Library, 2010), 183.

Second, unbelievers who hear sermons do not know how to respond to the Gospel apart from receiving instruction through an evangelistic invitation (e.g., Luke 3:10-14; Acts 2:37; 16:30). Pastors' aim should emulate the desire of August Hermann Francke when he writes, "As far as I am concerned, I must preach that should someone hear me only once before he dies, he will have heard not just a part, but the entire way of salvation and in the proper way for it to take root in his heart."[35]

The inherent nature of both the Scriptures and the Gospel elicits a response on the part of those who hear it. Effective text-driven and/or expositional preachers who call sinners to salvation should not tack on generic and repetitive invitations to the end of their sermons. Rather, their calls for sinners to repent and believe Christ should naturally flow from the text's own application.[36]

Although sermons serve as one, if not the most obvious, way for pastors to evangelize, pastors must not limit their evangelism to their sermons. They should also remind themselves that, in the New Testament, Jesus, Peter, Philip, and Paul alike evangelize both by their public preaching and through their personal conversations. Inasmuch as they sincerely desire to follow these New Testament paragons while seeking the lost from their pulpits, pastors should also convince themselves of the dual necessity in seeking the lost on the pavement.[37]

Do you present the Gospel in such a way when you preach that your hearers realize they have a decision to make? Or, do they leave from your sermons indifferent and unaware of their responsibility to receive the forgiveness of sins, reconciliation with the Father, eternal life, and the indwelling of the Holy Spirit by believing in Christ for salvation and repenting of their sins? Do you invite sinners to receive Christ with the exact same words and "pitch" when preaching from the Old Testament that you do preaching

---

[35]Paulus Scharpff, *History of Evangelism: Three Hundred Years of Evangelism in Germany, Great Britain, and the Unites States of America.* Helga Bender Henry, trans. (Grand Rapids: Eerdmans, 1966), 46.
[36]Queen, "Seeking the Lost and Perishing," 151.
[37]Ibid., 147-148.

from the New Testament? In other words, does the text you preach inform and influence your articulation of the public invitation, or do you say the same thing at the end of every sermon? Do you abdicate your responsibility for personal witnessing because of your public preaching? Write any changes you need to make in your delivery of public invitations in the **EVANGELISTIC PREACHING STRATEGIC ACTIONS** workspace.

EVANGELISTIC PREACHING STRATEGIC ACTIONS

8. Evangelistic Prayer

Refer to the responses to *Pastor Assessment Questionnaire* questions 12 and 19; *Ministry Staff/Lay Leader Assessment Questionnaire* question 12; and *Church Member Assessment Questionnaire* question

10 as you read and consider any strategic actions you need to plan and implement to improve your church's evangelistic praying.

Privately Praying Over Your Preaching

Question 19 of the *Pastor Assessment Questionnaire* asked, "If you offer some form of a public invitation, how much time each week do you dedicate to the public invitation in your sermon preparation?" If you do offer a public invitation as a part of your sermon, do you spend any time, during your sermon preparation, praying over the Gospel invitation you will issue on Sunday morning? Do you pray that God's Spirit will empower you to preach and convict sinners to repent?

C.H. Spurgeon attributed the overwhelming evangelistic responses in his meetings to his sermons being bathed in prayer. He told those he was training for ministry:

> ...[W]e must pray over our preaching. ... [N]o one can use the Gospel hammer well except he is much on his knees, but the Gospel hammer soon splits flinty hearts when a man knows how to pray. Prevail with God, and you will prevail with men. Straight from the closet to the pulpit let us come, with the anointing of God's Spirit fresh upon us. What we receive in secrecy we are cheerfully to dispense in public. Let us never venture to speak for God to men, until we have spoken for men to God.[38]

Spurgeon knew, however, that not all pastors earnestly prayed for sinners who would hear their sermons to be saved. He wrote, "[B]rethren, I think that those sermons which have been prayed over are the most likely to convert people. I mean those discourses that have had much real prayer offered over them, both in the preparation and the delivery, for there is much so-called prayer that is only playing at praying."[39]

---

[38] Spurgeon, *The Soul Winner*, 212-213.
[39] Ibid., 83.

In addition to praying for their own preaching, Spurgeon also encouraged preachers to enlist others to pray for them and their sermons, as well as to reach their friends through personal evangelism. He continued:

> It may happen that some of you do preach very earnestly and well, and sermons that are likely to be blessed, and yet you do not see sinners saved. Well, do not leave off preaching; but say to yourself, "I must try to gather around me a number of people who will be all praying with me and for me, and who will talk to their friends about the things of God, and who will so live and labour that the Lord will give a blessed shower of grace because all the surroundings are suitable thereto, and help to make the blessing come."[40]

Do you take time during your sermon preparation to pray for sinners to be convicted upon hearing the Word of God in order that they may receive Christ? If not, how could you incorporate such a prayer time in your sermon preparation? Do you encourage others to pray that unbelievers may be saved as a result of your sermon preparation and delivery? If so, whom do you encourage? If not, whom could you begin to enlist? Write your answers to these questions in the **EVANGELISTIC PRAYER STRATEGIC ACTIONS** workspace.

Corporately Praying for the Lost by Name

In addition to praying privately for unbelievers to be saved in your morning worship services, churches should corporately pray for the salvation of unbelievers by name. Studies conducted in the last 20 years consistently have found that churches considered most effective in their evangelism publicly pray for the salvation of unbelievers by name. Thom Rainer found that while the intensity and frequency of prayer in the evangelistic churches he studied

---

[40] Ibid., 107.

were commendable, equally noteworthy was the type of prayers offered corporately by the churches. He wrote, "Repeatedly pastors, staff, and laypersons told me that their churches prayed for the lost by name."[41] In a study among Georgia Baptists over a decade later, Steve Parr, Steve Foster, David Harrill, and Tom Crites discovered the same findings. The effective evangelistic churches they studied emphasized that they specifically identified and prayed for the lost by name.[42]

Consider leading your congregation to intercede publicly for the salvation of their lost family members, neighbors, friends, and co-workers. When leading your congregation in corporate prayer for unbelievers, you must exercise wisdom and sensitivity so as not to embarrass the unbelievers for whom you are praying. Precede such a prayer time with an explanation that churches must pray for all people, regardless of their spiritual condition, and to do otherwise would not be compassionate and caring. If you lead a corporate prayer during your worship services, petition the Lord to save your church members' unbelieving loved ones, inviting members of the congregation to call out a lost loved one's first name. You could also "enlist members who became believers as a result of the consistent public prayers and personal witness of church members to lead in these public prayer times as a testimony to this practice."[43]

Another way to pray corporately for the lost by name is to have your members utilize a tool like The Village Church Institute's *Evangelism Journal Workbook* (see Appendix 1). This workbook is a component of the church's overall training program, and it specifically asks members to identify persons they intend to evangelize and recount (1) why they are burdened for these specific people, (2) what they know about these people, and (3) the content of previous conversations with these people.

---

[41] Rainer, *Effective Evangelistic Churches*, 76.
[42] Parr, Foster, Harrill, and Crites, *Georgia's Top Evangelistic Churches*, 10.
[43] Queen, "Seeking the Lost and Perishing," 150-151.

For seven weeks, the members enter into the journal (1) a prayer for the salvation of those they have identified whom they intend to evangelize, (2) a plan by which they intend to interact with the people whom they have committed to evangelize, and (3) a summary explaining the details of that week's evangelistic interaction.

Are you intentionally leading your congregation to pray for the salvation of the lost by name? If so, in what ways, if any, could you improve? If not, what are some ways you can begin to lead them in these kinds of prayers? Use the **EVANGELISTIC PRAYER STRATEGIC ACTIONS** workspace to record some of your ideas.

EVANGELISTIC PRAYER
STRATEGIC ACTIONS

9. Evangelistic Training

Refer to the responses to *Pastor Assessment Questionnaire* questions 5 and 6 as you read and consider any strategic actions you need to plan and implement concerning evangelistic training.

Is Evangelism Training Really Necessary?

Seventeen years ago, David Beck, a New Testament and Greek professor at Southeastern Baptist Theological Seminary, used his sabbatical to address his concern that "[e]vangelism is often recognized as the heartbeat of the church, yet it is rarely the focus of serious research among biblical scholars." Upon his return, he gave a faculty lecture during a Southeastern chapel service on November 6, 2002. He asked faculty and students:

> How did people in the first century [evangelize] without attending an evangelism training seminar? Did Paul invent the FAITH outline, did Peter ever go through CWT, and did James write the Four Spiritual Laws booklet? ... Why did none of the New Testament authors write and circulate an evangelism how-to manual? ... It would seem that evangelism was not something planned or programmed by the early church. Yet consistently and constantly, "The Lord was adding to their number day by day those who were being saved [Acts 2:47]."[44]

He concluded that the early church does not appear "to have been trained in any special [evangelism] seminar. ... Evangelism in the life of the early church was neither a plan, program, or [sic] particular presentation. Rather, it was the natural overflow of hearts filled with Jesus."[45] So, in one sense, the Gospel your church members heard when they first believed is the only evangelism training they should ever need. In most churches,

---

[44] David R. Beck, "Evangelism in Luke-Acts: More Than an Outreach Program," *Faith & Mission* 20, no. 2 (Spring 2003): 85.
[45] Ibid., 86.

however, members do not feel as though they have received enough training to evangelize confidently.

Why Evangelism Training Seems Necessary

Evangelism training possesses many benefits beyond the confidence it offers church members to believe they have the necessary knowledge base and equipping tools to evangelize. It also creates an atmosphere within a congregation in which evangelism is valued and celebrated. Thom Rainer's groundbreaking research on effective evangelistic churches in 1996 found that a "significant reason for using evangelism training is the evangelistic attitude it engenders throughout the church. ... [It reinforces a message to the congregation] that the leadership of [the] church holds evangelism as a high priority."[46] If church members learn that a pastor and his staff value evangelism, they typically will embrace and prioritize evangelism over time.

In addition to the confidence it gives and atmosphere it creates, the availability of evangelism training to a congregation also results in measureable effectiveness. When Steve Parr and Tom Crites asked Georgia Baptist churches in 2011 whether they provided evangelism training to their members in the past 12 months, the results were as follows:

Response	% Response	Average Baptisms	Worship Attendees to Baptism Ratio
No	52%	6.2	18.7 to 1
Yes	48%	16.0	15.5 to 1

As they reported: "[T]he churches that provide[d] personal evangelism training baptized 20.6% more than those that did not provide training, when viewing from the perspective of ratios of attendees to baptisms. They baptized almost three times as

---

[46] Rainer, *Effective Evangelistic Churches*, 39.

many when viewing as a cumulative total."[47] Another study they conducted further verified the congregational effectiveness of utilizing evangelism training:

> [In 2008] Georgia's churches were asked on [their] Annual Church Profile to report their method(s) for training their members in personal evangelism. The results revealed that only 23% provided evangelism training to their members. ... By contrast, 87% of [those who were identified as] the top evangelistic churches [in Georgia] intentionally provided personal evangelism training for their members in the [previous] year. A similar result occurred a few years ago when the Sunday School/Open Group Ministries of the Georgia Baptist Convention studied the 100 fastest growing Sunday Schools. Eighty-five percent of the churches in that study provided personal evangelism training. Coincidence? That is not likely, given the prevalence of the responses. In addition, the churches were asked, "What is your most effective way of engaging members in personal evangelism?" The most frequent answer by an overwhelming margin was "providing personal evangelism training."[48]

Clearly, evangelism training affords a pastor numerous benefits in his pursuit to mobilize his congregation to evangelize.

The Pastor, the Staff or Member Evangelist, and Evangelistic Training

C.B. Hogue explains that training, coupled with preaching, assists a pastor to mobilize his people: "Motivation through preaching is useless without training through teaching; the pastor must work alongside—and yet through—the lay persons in his

---

[47] Parr and Crites, *Evangelistic Effectiveness*, 35.
[48] Parr, Foster, Harrill, and Crites, *Georgia's Top Evangelistic Churches*, 8-9.

church, or he will never fulfill the intent of his own ministry."[49] A pastor may find that the demand of his duties prevents him from being able to train his people in evangelism as much as he desires. He must teach his people to evangelize, but he should not be the only one teaching his people to evangelize. Employing a vocational evangelist on his staff, or utilizing grace-gifted evangelists whom the pastor has identified within his congregation, will prove to be both an efficient and effective means to provide evangelism training, as long as the pastor continues to lead his congregation to evangelize. As I state elsewhere:

> Churches that desire the total participation of their membership in evangelism will employ a vocational or voluntary staff evangelist for the purpose of equipping and encouraging evangelism. In churches that do so, pastors must overcome any temptation to abdicate their evangelistic leadership among the congregation to the evangelist. No matter how much charisma, giftedness, and respect staff evangelists may possess, congregations ultimately follow the headship and example of their lead pastors. Thus, even as all believers are responsible for reaching the lost, the pastor must model that obedience for those with whom he serves. The most effective and consistent churches who seek the lost and perishing utilize ministry teams that include pastors who champion evangelism and employ the assistance of staff evangelists who equip and encourage evangelism under the direction of their shepherd.[50]

Not every pastor will be a grace-gifted evangelist, but every pastor should be a Spirit-empowered, personal evangelist who promotes and teaches evangelism to his people.

---

[49] Hogue, *I Want My Church to Grow*, 71.
[50] Queen, "Seeking the Lost and Perishing," 148.

Evangelism Training Made Easy[51]

How might the members of your church be taught to present the Gospel from the natural overflow of their hearts that are filled with Jesus? Perhaps such a transition would occur if they were taught to shift from reciting their latest memorized Gospel outline to recalling the Gospel they first heard in order to believe. One way this kind of evangelism can be possible begins by asking them, in the context of a formal session of evangelism training, to answer three questions:

A. What are the Gospel essentials?

What content must a personal evangelist communicate in order to share the entire Gospel with unbelievers? Recall Paul's summary of the Gospel: "For I delivered to you as of first importance what I also received, that Christ died for our sins according to the Scriptures, and that He was buried, and that He was raised on the third day according to the Scriptures" (1 Corinthians 15:3-4).

Anyone who knows enough of the Gospel to have heard it, believed it, and been saved by it, knows enough of the Gospel to share it. Conversely, anyone who does not know enough of the Gospel to share it should ask himself whether he has ever heard and believed enough of the Gospel to have been saved by it in the first place.

Recall the Gospel message you heard and believed. At its core, it likely included (1) the reality and consequences of sin; (2) the truth that the God-man Jesus Christ died for your sins, was buried, and was raised on the third day; and (3) an invitation to repent of your sins; believe Jesus' death, burial, and resurrection alone saves you; and verbally confess, "Jesus is Lord."

Although your recollection of the Gospel's core elements may be worded or enumerated differently, find encouragement that you

---

[51] Taken from Matt Queen, "Toward a 'By the Book' and a 'From the Heart' Kind of Evangelism," March 13, 2018; https://theologicalmatters.com/2018/03/13/toward-a-by-the-book-and-from-the-heart-kind-of-evangelism/.

already know the Gospel and can share it naturally with unbelievers who need to hear it.

B. What Scriptures will I use to communicate these essentials?

Which Scriptures communicate these essentials you heard and believed? The New Testament presents two reasons why the Scriptures must be incorporated into our Gospel presentations. First, hearing the Word of Christ is prerequisite for biblical faith. Paul wrote, "So faith comes from hearing, and hearing by the word of Christ" (Romans 10:17). Second, evangelistic proclamations in the New Testament overwhelmingly incorporate the Scriptures (e.g., Luke 24:14-32; Acts 2:14-41; 3:11-26; 4:1-12; 7; 8:4, 35; 13:13-49; 16:25-32; 17:10-13; 18:5, 28; 20:27; 26:22-23; 28:23-27).

Likely you can call to mind verses that, in their immediate context and with their intended meaning, communicate the Gospel essentials you heard and believed. For example, Romans 3:23 communicates the consequences and reality of sin. 1 Corinthians 15:3-4 conveys the truth that the God-man Jesus Christ died for your sins, was buried, and raised on the third day. And Romans 10:9 conveys the Gospel's invitation to repent of your sins; believe in Jesus Christ and His death, burial, and resurrection for your salvation; and verbally confess, "Jesus is Lord."

With the Spirit's help, select a verse that communicates each of the Gospel essentials you have already identified. Now, utilize these verses in your evangelistic presentation of those Gospel essentials.

C. How will I instruct a willing hearer to repent, believe, and confess?

Some Christians believe that the most nervous aspect about evangelism comes at the beginning of the process—starting a Gospel conversation with another person. However, another aspect of evangelism can be just as terrifying, if not more so—finding that the person you evangelize is simultaneously convicted by God's

Spirit, yet you do not know how to help him receive Christ. How will you lead an unbeliever to repent of his sins, believe in Jesus Christ for salvation, and confess Him as Lord?

If, after an unbeliever hears the Gospel and is convicted by the Spirit, you are convinced that he genuinely desires to repent, believe, and confess, then consider asking him to call on God in prayer. Usually, an unbeliever does not know how to pray to God. So, first have him articulate in prayer the reason he finds himself praying to God. Generally, you are listening for him to admit his sinfulness and need for God's forgiveness. Second, ask him to tell God, in his own words, that what he has understood from the Gospel essentials you shared can forgive his sins and make him right with God. Listen for him to reference the essence of the Gospel. Third, instruct him to confess with sincerity the phrase, "Jesus is Lord." Last, invite him to thank God for what he understands God has done for him. Usually, new believers will thank God for His forgiveness, His presence, His mercy, and His grace.

Do you ensure your church has access to consistent evangelism training? If so, what training do you make available to them? Have you experienced similar evangelistic results to those reported by churches in Georgia? If your church does not offer periodic evangelism training, how could you begin to do so? How can you teach your people evangelism? Do you know of a vocational or volunteer evangelist you could utilize? Write your responses in the **EVANGELISTIC TRAINING STRATEGIC ACTIONS** workspace.

EVANGELISTIC TRAINING
STRATEGIC ACTIONS

NEED FURTHER HELP?

If you would like help in mobilizing your congregation for effective evangelism, please contact me at MQueen@swbts.edu or (817) 923-1921, extension 6480.

BIBLIOGRAPHY

Autrey, C.E. *Basic Evangelism*. Grand Rapids: Zondervan, 1959.

Baldwin, Jonathan. "Who Can Do the Work? A Biblical Examination of the Work of an Evangelist in 2 Timothy 4:1-15." Ph.D. Seminar Paper, Southwestern Baptist Theological Seminary, 2017.

Drummond, Lewis A. *Leading Your Church in Evangelism*. Nashville: Broadman, 1975.

Fink, Roger and Rodney Stark. *The Churching of America, 1776-2005: Winners and Losers in Our Religious Economy*. Rev. ed. Piscataway: Rutgers University Press, 2005.

Hartman, Warren J. *Membership Trends: A Study of the Decline and Growth in the United Methodist Church 1949-1975*. Nashville: Discipleship Resources, 1976.

Hesselgrave, David J. *Paradigms in Conflict*. Grand Rapids: Kregel, 2005.

Hoge, Dean R. "A Test of Theories of Denominational Growth and Decline." *Understanding Church Growth and Decline 1950-1978*. Edited by Dean R. Hoge and David A. Roozen. New York: Pilgrim Press, 1979.

Hogue, C.B. *I Want My Church to Grow*. Nashville: Broadman, 1977.

Kelley, Charles S., Jr. *How Did They Do It: The Story of Southern Baptist Evangelism*. N.C.: Insight Press, 1993.

Kelly, Dean. *Why Conservative Churches are Growing*. New York: Harper & Row, 1972.

McKinney, William J., Jr. "Performance of United Church of Christ Congregations in Massachusetts and Pennsylvania." *Understanding Church Growth and Decline 1950-1978*. Edited by Dean R. Hoge and David A. Roozen. New York: Pilgrim Press, 1979.

Morgan, G. Campbell. *Evangelism*. East Northfield: The Bookstore, 1904.

Oldham, Roger S. "Annual Church Profile Gives Church, SBC 'Report Cards.'" Accessed March 13, 2018. https://brnow.org/News/July-2014/Annual-Church-Profile-gives-churches-SBC-report-ca.

Parr, Steve R., Steve Foster, David Harrill, and Tom Crites. *Georgia's Top Evangelistic Churches: Ten Lessons from the Most Effective Churches*. Duluth: Georgia Baptist Convention, 2008.

_____ and Thomas Crites. *Evangelistic Effectiveness: A Research Report*. Duluth: Baxter Press, 2012.

Pipes, Carol. "Southern Baptists Report More Churches in 2016; Baptism, Membership Decline." Accessed March 13, 2018. https://blog.lifeway.com/newsroom/2017/06/08/southern-baptists-report-more-churches-in-2016-baptisms-membership-decline/.

Pruitt, Shane. "Awaiting Gospel Preaching: Should Church Members Expect the Gospel in Every Sermon?" April 11, 2018. http://preachingsource.com/blog/awaiting-gospel-preaching-should-church-members-expect-the-gospel-in-every-sermon/.

Queen, Matt. "Evangelism is Not a Spiritual Gift." April 4, 2017. http://theologicalmatters.com/2017/04/04/do-some-believers-possess-a-spiritual-gift-of-evangelism-or-do-all-believers-receive-the-holy-spirit-in-order-to-evangelize/.

_____. "Seeking the Lost and Perishing." *Pastoral Ministry: The Ministry of a Shepherd*, Edited by Deron Biles. Nashville: B&H Academic, 2018.

_____. "Toward a 'By the Book' and a 'From the Heart' Kind of Evangelism." March 13, 2018. https://theologicalmatters. com/2018/03/13/toward-a-by-the-book-and-from-the-heart-kind-of-evangelism/.

Rainer, Thom. *Effective Evangelistic Churches*. Nashville: Broadman, 1996.

Reid, Alvin. *Evangelism Handbook: Biblical, Spiritual, Intentional, Missional*. Nashville: B&H, 2009.

Rommen, Edward. *Get Real: On Evangelism in the Late Modern World*. Pasadena: William Carey Library, 2010.

Scharpff, Paulus. *History of Evangelism: Three Hundred Years of Evangelism in Germany, Great Britain, and the Unites States of America*. Translated by Helga Bender Henry. Grand Rapids: Eerdmans, 1966.

Skelton, Eugene. *Ten Fastest Growing Southern Baptist Sunday Schools*. Nashville: Broadman, 1975.

Spurgeon, C.H. *The Soul Winner*. London: Passmore & Alabaster, 1895.

Stott, John R.W. *Guard the Gospel: The Message of 2 Timothy*. Downers Grove: InterVarsity Press, 1973.

Wagner, C. Peter. *Leading Your Church to Growth*. Ventura: Regal, 1984.

Whitesell, Faris Daniel. *Basic New Testament Evangelism*. Grand Rapids: Zondervan, 1949.

APPENDIX

Evangelism Journal Workbook[52]

The Village Church Institute
TRAINING PROGRAM

Christian Formation Assignment: Practicing Evangelism

"How then will they call on him in whom they have not believed? And how are they to believe in him of whom they have never heard? And how are they to hear without someone preaching? And how are they to preach unless they are sent? As it is written, 'How beautiful are the feet of those who preach the good news!'" (Rom. 10:14-15)

Sharing the gospel can be one of the most intimidating aspects of the Christian life. And yet, the Lord has called us to do the joy of proclaiming the gospel to people who have not yet believed upon Christ Jesus.

Assignment: Over the next 7 weeks we are asking that every Training Program participant explicitly share the gospel with a non-Christian in their life. This could be a friend, co-worker, family member, neighbor, or someone you providentially encounter going about your days.

By "explicitly share the gospel" we mean: That you explain to them the good news of Christ Jesus and make an appeal to them to repent and place their faith in Him.

In order to keep track of how this goes, and to hold us all accountable, we are asking that you will record one prayer and one intentional interaction with this person each week. We are providing you with a workbook that you can use. We strongly encourage you to practice presenting the gospel with a person in your cohort before trying this with the non-Christian person you hope to share it with.

We also have some suggested resources that may help you as you prepare to share the gospel with this person in a way that is both concise and compelling.

Suggested Resources:
* Two Ways to Live
* The Story
* The Bridge Illustration

---

[52]Used by permission of Kyle Worley and the Village Church Institute. Following is an example of one of the seven weekly journals members of the Training Institute are asked to complete.

EVANGELISM JOURNAL WORKBOOK

Your name:

Person You Plan to Share Gospel With:

Why you are burdened for this person:

Where do you normally see this person:

What do you know about them (interests, family, fears, personality):

What have you talked about with them previously?

WEEK ONE

Prayer:

I plan to interact with this person in the following way this week:

How did that interaction go: